The Energy to Teach

Donald H. Graves

Heinemann
Portsmouth, NH

44979651

3/03

Heinemann
A division of Reed Elsevier Inc.
361 Hanover Street
Portsmouth, NH 03801-3912
www.heinemann.com

Offices and agents throughout the world

Copyright © 2001 by Donald H. Graves.

Library of Congress Cataloging-in-Publication Data
Graves, Donald H.
The energy to teach / Donald H. Graves.
p. cm.
Includes bibliographical references (p.).
ISBN 0-325-00326-2 (alk. paper)
1. Effective teaching. 2. Teachers—Psychology. 3. Teachers—Job satisfaction. I. Title.

LB10253.3 .G73 2001
371.102—dc21

00-046199

Editor: Lois Bridges
Cover art: Georgia Heard
Cover design: Judy Arisman
Back cover photo: Kucine Photography
Manufacturing: Louise Richardson

Printed in the United States of America on acid-free paper
06 05 04 03 02 VP 10 9 8 7 6

To Betty
Where energy begins

Contents

Acknowledgments

The idea for *The Energy to Teach* began with the last chapter of *Bring Life into Learning*. I was very much aware of what brought life into learning but the contrast of much of the fatigue in the profession with the promised energy in curriculum led me to begin an eighteen-month journey of extensive interviews in person, on the Internet, and through informal conversations.

I owe a special debt to my editor, Lois Bridges, for both books. Lois has the most extensive vocabulary I know surrounding the word *encouragement*. Lois has an unlimited range of encouraging words that she uses with precision. She doesn't duck the places in the text that lack clarity. Somehow, she sees possibilities in these problems that make me want to go back to work immediately. I shall forever be grateful to her for bringing life to my retirement years.

Maura Sullivan from marketing at Heinemann is always encouraging. She has a unique gift for taking books about a wide range of subjects and stating succinctly the essence of those books. I can't afford to ignore the penetrating questions that Maura asks. I am grateful to her for helping me and others to focus and produce good work.

Many people helped with this book whose names I cannot mention. I had to assure my interviewees complete anonymity. They had to feel free to speak frankly about their teaching and administrative circumstances. Truly, these are the unsung heroes of this study and I am in debt to them. Within the large group of people I interviewed is a special group of six informants. We maintained dialogue over much longer periods of time through personal telephone interviews and via the Internet. They kept detailed notes and conducted research on themselves and their use of time. This study is quite dependent on their detailed note taking.

I thank another group of people outside the profession. In order to gain a comparative picture of energy in the workplace I interviewed doctors, chief executive officers, small-business people, realtors, office managers, students and professors in universities. They provided a needed perspective on energy issues in the workplace that allowed me to see what other occupations have in common with educators. I am grateful to them for helping me with this study.

Virginia Secor in Chapter 11, "A Portrait in Energy," captured the meaning of professional energy and was a valuable guide to me in much of my thinking. In addition, a large number of educators in Maine were especially helpful in giving me details about their approach to vision making in the state. Professor Brenda Power made me aware of the high-quality work in the state, provided responses to my work, and opened doors to people who might be interviewed for this study.

I am grateful to Anna Sumida, from Kamehameha School in Hawaii, who read each of the chapters and provided valuable responses. Others read different chapters: Sally Swenson, Camille Allen, Jane Hansen, Danling Fu, Wendy Murray from *Scholastic Books*, and Sharon Lundahl from Maryland.

Although not reading texts directly, Bobbi Fisher and Regie Routman were always ready to discuss ideas about energy. I am grateful for their encouragement. Shelley Harwayne, who has that inexhaustible supply of energy, and somehow unlocks it in children, parents, and teachers, was an inspiration for this book. Indeed, she is an example of the type of educator with whom I needed to discuss the profession. Shelley's book, *Going Public*, is a portrait of an energy-filled school.

Sometimes in late afternoon I'd phone Diane Levin from the California State Department of Education. I'd call for an "energy fix" and we'd discuss the current state of energy in the profession. Diane read many of the chapters in this book and provided cogent comment. Discussions with Diane on any subject lead to new angles for increasing energy. Diane reminds me how important it is to laugh at the pretensions in our profession.

I have daily conversations with two people who have contributed greatly to this book. I chat with Don Murray about the New England Patriots and Boston Red Sox, old age, and especially the gift of life. We have been talking about writing, the world, and life for nearly thirty years. I read his column, "Over 60," in the *Boston Globe* to maintain my bearings. I am not afraid to sign my letters to him, "With love." I call Dorothy Lowry every morning at 7:45. We've talked daily for two and one half years since her diagnosis with multiple myeloma. She asks, "What are you going to do today?" And I answer, "I'm going to write this morning." Of course, we go on to discuss other things, local news, cancer treatments, travel. I am grateful to her for her perspective on life, her friendship, and the every-day summoning up of energy for the day ahead.

I am grateful to my friend and colleague, Georgia Heard, for her work on the cover of this book. Georgia is best known as a poet and extraordinary teacher. Few know her as an artist. When I saw the cover she painted for her own book I hoped that she might do the one for *the Energy to Teach*. I think her designs and colors have captured the energy feeling.

Renée Le Verrier has gone the final mile in bringing this book to successful publication. There are endless details from layout to final edits, as well as coordination of all the people who bring a book to press. She does this with grace and intelligence.

The actual idea for this book came at the end of a six-mile run with Maggie Solomon on November 12, 1998. I asked her, "What gives you energy and what takes it away?" Maggie, the epitome of the high-energy person, quickly gave me her list and urged me to keep asking the question. I am grateful for her encouragement.

Dr. Rob Richardson, a psychiatrist, and I have walked together every Wednesday for the past three years. We talk theory and articles. He shares theoretical schemes, poetry, and short writes and I pass my articles to him. He has been most encouraging about the energy study and has asked a number of tough questions about some of my observations. I am grateful to him for his patience and understanding as we've discussed energy questions for a solid year and one half. It seems that everything we discuss is related to energy.

My dear wife, Betty, has walked with me through this book and the other twenty books I've written. She is my first reader. When she doesn't understand a text, I listen. I have learned from her that one of the great energy sources is companionship. We work on flower beds, cut trees, hike trails, cycle, travel in the car to our children and grandchildren. I've noticed that I don't write as well on days she is away from Jackson, N.H. She contributes by just "being there" in the house. I'll never take that for granted. This book is dedicated to Betty.

A Word from the Artist

I love the idea of renewal and how, as a teacher, artist, and mother, my job is to renew my vision—to see again as if for the first time whether it's the world, the students I teach, or my son. And this re-visioning helps to sustain me and gives me back energy. For the cover of Don's book, which I was so honored to be asked to create, I wanted to paint both light and renewal. I closed my eyes and thought of all the love and energy Don has given me and all of us, and how he's given me the energy to teach. I opened my heart and let my hand lead me to this painting of fire and water, light and renewal.

—Georgia Heard
Writer, Artist

Freddy

Until that moment,
ferret-faced Freddy
ruined my days. Eggs sat
cold on my morning plate,
the weather cloudy and grey,
and when I turned out
the light I heard
him laugh, "I wasn't doin'
nothin', Mr. Graves."

But on that day
when with eyes
lit by a new fire he asked,
"Did you know
Humpback pods create
a new song each year?"
something jumped between us.

We each built new lives
on that simple question;
Freddy followed his whales
and I've been looking
for what kids know
ever since.

Don Graves

1

The Energy to Teach

An Emotional Roller Coaster

Teaching is an emotional roller coaster. In the space of eight hours and twenty-eight children you try to accommodate for two new students who arrive with no transfer papers, handle an explosion from a child who has just spent a weekend with his alcoholic father, or fight the interference of an imposing intercom when reading a story aloud to the class. At 9:30 you celebrate with Mark Chang who is captured by Gary Paulsen's *Hatchet*. "I'm going to finish this one," he says and you know it will be the first book he's ever read by himself.

You celebrate Mark's breakthrough with a colleague in the teacher's room, but Mary Gondolf overrides your story bemoaning the impending state assessments that will begin next Monday. Mary has a way of showering good news with cynicism. You usually avoid the teacher's room if Mary is in there alone because you know you will leave with less energy than when you entered. You pretend you've just come in to get a quick cup of coffee.

Word has trickled down from the Board, to superintendent, to principal, to you, the teacher: The administration wants you to give weekly writing prompts and promote daily skill builders and phonics in reading instruction. Every day a new pressure arrives at your classroom door. You feel as though you must buffer these demands for real, long-term learning for the children. Everyone seems to be in a hurry to deal with the crisis in education. The word *crisis* is used interchangeably with reading. When they speak of The Crisis you know what people mean. You know that invoking the crisis word means the usual suspension of professional judgment and the absence of respect. Outside consultants bring with them the news that they have surefire methodologies that are teacher-proof. Plug in and see the scores rise. Their graphs and charts show that this district, like all the others they've visited, have demolished the national norms. You begin to feel a general weariness and a dull headache. You push the surefire methods back into your subconscious and get on with teaching.

You take a field trip to the beach in the afternoon where you investigate tide pools. Silent Martha who seldom speaks is chatting away like a magpie and won't leave your side. This day the children are recording the various organisms in the tide pools. They shout their discoveries and add to their lists. Ben Yadow has discovered a starfish spreading open a clam. A crowd soon gathers. Though the drama is slow the children are fascinated by the power of the starfish's suction cups. "Gross, awesome!" they shout. Wise Ben says, "Pretty soon he'll be lowering his stomach into the clam to eat." And you say, "This is why I want to teach."

Every day you and millions of teachers walk into rooms across the country to teach. You are instructor, teacher, supervisor, parent, and project director. Most of all you are teacher/parent. In the course of a year you will spend over a thousand hours with the children and experience the full range of emotions associated with parenting. You will demand, cajole, nudge, rejoice, celebrate, despair, weep, laugh, sermonize, and express anger. You will experience all the emotions of a parent who may have but one child. In your case you will have from twenty to thirty-five.

At times you will be second-guessed by parents, administrators, and pundits who have never taught. Laws will be passed that try to govern the teaching transactions you make with children. You will observe that the volume of rhetoric by the experts is directly related to the distance the speaker is from the classroom.

The Purpose of This Book

As with supervisors in other occupations you cannot fire the children, lay them off, send them off on assignment, or ignore them. They are simply yours. And since they are yours you will ride the emotional roller coaster. Emotional roller coasters demand energy—high energy—and you need to know how to maximize what gives you energy and minimize what takes it away. You need to regain the energy to teach.

2

You will find new ways to take energy from students and parents and learn how to focus your work with curriculum. You will witness how colleagues give energy to each other and view several portraits of teachers with high energy. I will show from my own research how people in other occupations build energy into their own workplaces. Finally, I will review principles from the data that show how teachers can tap into more lasting sources of energy. You do have the power to make decisions that contribute to these sources. This book will help you to set a clear professional direction toward tapping those sources.

A New Study

As I've traveled around the country the last five years, I've noticed increased tension and fatigue in our profession. Teacher judgment is continually bypassed by legislatures, state departments of education, and local admnistrations who try to micromanage the transactions between teachers and children. There is an overemphasis on normed tests with built-in failure rates that have little to do with lasting learning. In most cases the achievement tests merely check aptitude for learning yet they are used as a sign of progress within school systems.

Tests are emphasized as ends in themselves rather than as indicators school systems need to consider for new directions. Sadly, there is less and less explanation and quest for a commonality of purpose based on shared visions within school systems. I notice that when hurry-up objectives are put in place with instruction directed toward the singular objective of higher test scores, teacher fatigue is the result. Teachers are asked to do more and more things in their classrooms that make no sense. One teacher expressed it best, "When I know that what I am doing wouldn't be good for my own child, I rebel." Teachers rebel but more often they feel mired in the malaise of no energy. Senseless work in the midst of high pressure is a prescription for significant energy loss, chronic absenteeism, and a discouraged profession.

Of course, not all teachers suffer from a lack of energy. Some are able to transcend the most difficult circumstances and foster significant learning in their students. There are also teachers who are part of a building or system with a clear vision for learning. They give energy to each other and continually transform goals to match their vision for children.

3

In the fall of 1998 I decided the energy problem in our profession was significant enough to study it. I began to interview elementary and secondary teachers, administrators, academics, students, and parents. The interview opened with one basic question: "Tell me what gives you energy, takes it away, and what for you is a waste of time." I interviewed people from Maine to Hawaii. Interviews averaged an hour in length and were often face to face. But I also interviewed a large number of teachers over the telephone and an even larger number via the Internet.

Six teachers volunteered for more extensive interviews, lasting several months. The interviews were more an exchange of views, analysis, and written reflection. At one point I asked each to make a note of everything they did at home and at school over seven days. They then noted which activity or event was energy giving, taking, or what seemed to be a waste of time.

I also wanted to interview people in other professions and occupations using the same basic question. The interviews generally lasted about one hour and in some instances there were follow-up meetings. I thought that the nature of energy demands in teaching, as well as solutions, could best be handled through a comparative review.

Although there are issues leading to energy drain in our profession, this book will focus more on solutions. I have learned from my study participants what they do to increase their energy or deal with possible energy-depleting problems.

Teachers Speak About Energy Drain

Lack of Control over Time and Space

Although learning is the concern of all, often the very people who espouse its importance unwittingly do little to protect teaching time. Listen to this fifth-grade teacher in a suburban school:

> I call it harassment. Anyone can walk into my room and interrupt me with notes, come over the loudspeaker system, or change my schedule with only a few minutes notice. The same people who want to have better scores on tests are the same people who keep turning things upside down. I want to teach and it makes me angry when this goes on. And when I'm angry afterwards my energy drops to zero.

Anthropologists are interested in who controls time and space in a society. Some cultures have elaborate systems of permissions when there is an interruption in what is most valued in a society. If we say that instruction is the most important activity that occurs in a school then teachers ought to have greater control of their time and space. At the least there should be active consultation concerning any change in how teachers are managing instruction. A closed classroom door and a closed door to the principal's office require different sets of permissions for anyone to enter. In the teacher's case no permission is required but the principal's office, the visitor or teacher must consult with the secretary before being allowed admittance.

Lack of Support

In addition to lack of control over time and space, energy loss begins with a general sense of meaninglessness expressed as, "What are we doing this for anyway?" When there is distance between the rhetoric of school improvement and the lack of a common vision within a system, a sense of purpose is lost as well as the energy to teach. Confusion and a lack of common vision soon grow into resentment, then anger. Although it may feel good to vent one's anger, the anger, if not directed toward solution, leads to serious energy loss.

When administrators don't back teachers, or at least explain why they can't, and there is a clear conflict of values, energy is depleted. This sixth-grade teacher in a semi-urban class expressed it this way:

> I have a few guidelines that children must follow in my room. One of them is simply being respectful of each other. Well, I uncovered a ring of nasty notes that three girls were passing around about one of the children who is overweight. I called the three girls on it and we sat down and had a good frank talk about it. I wanted them to appreciate how that poor girl felt. Next thing you know the mothers of those girls went to the principal and we all had a meeting. The upshot is that the principal didn't back what I'd done. She said that I was overreacting to something that is quite normal for girls to do at that age. It may be normal but I'm not about to let that kind of behavior go by. They need to know the effect of what they are doing. I confess that I'm so tired at the end of days like that. You know, I find that anger and fatigue walk hand in hand.

Once again, there is not only a conflict of values, but an overruling of a teacher who sets very definite standards.

Difficult Children

Finally, dealing with difficult children can be an energy drain. There are two types of difficult situations with children. The first type is the child who simply can't control emotional outbursts. The class tries to function, knowing that at any moment something unpredictable will happen with this one child. The next type is the child with a range of both home and school problems. The teacher can already see how the deck is stacked against the child. The child is constantly absent, shows a little potential, yet the family situation dictates future failure in school and society. The reflective practitioner sees the implications of the child's school trajectory, yet feels helpless in reversing the outcome. Both the teacher and the child feel a sense of futility.

Teachers Speak About What Gives Them Energy

I note two large sources of energy in teachers' lives: the students, and a sense of collegiality with other teachers.

> There's nothing quite like being there the moment a child says, "I can read. I can read."

Most of us went into teaching to help our students learn. It is no surprise then when evidence of a child's learning is a significant energy giver. I suspect that in one single day, there are literally thousands of learning stories and episodes that are unfolding in schools around the country. We need to know how to release them for ourselves and the children.

The Students

Quite by accident, I stumbled on to a child who showed me how to get good learning stories. I was a researcher in Mary Ellen Giacobbe's first-grade classroom at the time. One boy, Scott, was writing a story about sliding down a hill and he put a period at the end of the sentence. I hadn't seen him do that before. "Scott," I asked, "You put that period in just the right place. How did you know how to do that?"

6

"Well, if I didn't put the period there, the kid would have slid right into the house," he replied. I've been asking children why they get certain things right ever since. I confess that before that incident I'd usually put my finger on an error saying, "You got that wrong, Scott. How come?" I find that children are much more expansive with answers and imagination when they know they are on firm ground at the outset. Sometimes their answers appear out of context because they have no idea how or why something is accurate. When I do tell them more precisely why something is accurate, I usually have their full attention.

Colleagues

Teachers frequently refer to colleagues as energy givers. Next to children, this was most often cited in the interviews. Here are some examples of ways colleagues help:

> We have a librarian in our school who is so selfless and helpful that just walking in there and out again gives me energy. Sometimes I just walk through to get a lift.

> Certain people fuel me like Bill Allen, my colleague with whom I discuss poetry almost daily; we allow each other the power of an identity other than the teacher we both know we are to each other and we give permission to be the poets we both call ourselves.

> I get energy from being asked for advice. It is quite a compliment, a kind of life force, when someone asks your professional opinion. At a faculty meeting after school the staff expressed concern and solicited my opinion about the very large anticipated enrollment next year. We may have as many as 35 in the fifth grade next year.

Long-term, established relationships with other teachers are often taken for granted unless specific questions direct respondents in that direction. One teacher reported:

> I get energy when I eat with the faculty. We talk lots about our families. I realize that in the two years I have been at the school, I have made good friends and enjoy the people I am able to work with—on a personal and professional level. I also went out to dinner with a group of friends/colleagues. We are a group who taught together several years ago, but for one reason or another, we are all in various schools.

7

This same teacher went on to speak about the necessity of leaving the school to come in contact with other educators:

> I think that much of my energy comes from other people—conversations, visits, meetings, books, etc. I am going to hear Anna Quindlen this week and I know her talk will be energizing. There is something special about inspiring people that gives me energy—something about certain people I connect with. You know, we need people we look up to just like anyone else.

One of the important principles for increasing energy is deliberately expanding the scope of professional contacts. Others reported engaging in chats with other teachers on the Internet. Both CATENET (California Association of Teachers of English) and NCTE (National Council of Teachers of English) provide help in this direction:

> Don't laugh but I get energy from e-mail. E-mail breaks the isolation and there are certain, reliable people I can share with, complain, pass along jokes. It's an instant quick fix and I'll never apologize for doing it. It works! I become part of a broader community of professionals. It's your instant NCTE or IRA.

When We Aren't Teaching in School

I asked my informants about what gives and takes away energy both in school and out. As much as we may try, it is virtually impossible to keep the two worlds apart. A mother who leaves her fussy two-year-old son at child care knows the tension of wondering how he is doing throughout her teaching day. Other teachers were concerned about older children dealing with the one- to two-hour gap at home alone before the teachers arrived home from school. Unexpected teacher meetings that extended the gap produced both tension and energy drain.

I asked what gave them energy outside of school. Their responses were varied:

> My wife, sometimes just from being with her, others from talking with her, still others from just thinking about her; she completes me, guides me, accompanies me; I have no equivalent friend nor any other who can fill me so full so fast.

I've realized for a long time that listening to music, and especially playing music or singing along energizes me and have often thought that I'm in some other world or another life—I create music all the time. When I was singing along with a tape on the way home, I realized how relaxed I was becoming and how freely my energy was flowing.

I had a relaxing breakfast with my husband and daughter. That wasn't an accident because I deliberately planned to have that time be right so I got up half an hour early and it worked. I knew I was getting off to school on the wrong foot and I got such an energy boost from it that it carried me through the day.

Sometimes the energy drains beyond school are particularly weighty. I asked a number of respondents the following question: "Tell me about three or four things that you've been carrying over the past five years that are particularly draining." Especially draining were divorce, children in trouble, a husband's drinking, a mother with Alzheimer's disease, a move to a new community, buying a home. In some cases teachers arrived at school already carrying significant burdens that took away energy.

A State Takes the Right Tack

Thanks to a chance remark by Brenda Power, professor at the University of Maine, I discovered an unusual source of energy. She'd just returned from a retreat on Mt. Desert Island off the coast of Maine. The State Department of Education examined the results of childrens' primary reading scores, and called in the systems producing the highest results and asked a simple question, "Would you mind telling us how you did it? What did you do to get such high scores?"

I sensed a very important energy principle at work. When things go well, ask people how they do it. States spend too much time with systems that are struggling without finding out the stories behind the systems that are doing well. Every system has something in it that is going well. Let's find out how they do it. It does not mean that problems are ignored, but they must be balanced against unusual and effective solutions. The Maine systems were quite surprised to find a wide range of approaches used to teach reading. What is consistent across those systems is informed, effective teamwork and leadership based on a common vision developed over many years. There were no dramatic, one-year turnarounds. Chapter 10 of this book tells more of the Maine story.

The Energy to Teach

We are embarking on a long journey that never ends. I am 69 years old as I write these words and I know I will continue on this search until the end of life itself. Indeed, it is the journey that counts, not the destination.

There are a few simple principles that I will borrow thanks to the gift of a book from a professional friend, Cindy Marten. I refer to *Seven Habits of Highly Effective People* by Stephen R. Covey (1989). The principles that I will develop further are proactivity and the notion of progressing from dependence to independence to interdependence. Simply put, we do have the power to break out of energy-depleting situations. We have the power to change our interpretations of events and make a difference to ourselves and the children we teach. We generate energy through knowledge, sound decisions, and self-discipline. We can choose to move away from being dependent on those who drain us, gain some independence, and move to the greatest energy giver of all, living, giving, and practicing in communities of mutual dependence and vision. The balance of our lives will have shifted from an emotional roller coaster to a more consistent source of energy and a clearer destination in mind.

This book will take us on a journey together through a series of invitations. The invitations will ask you to try things that produce motion toward the objectives you wish to achieve both personally and professionally. Many of these invitations come from my reading, personal practice, and what I have learned from my study participants. Enjoy the journey.

2

Taking Stock

I know that you already have a sense of what takes energy, gives it, and is a waste of time. What you need now are the specifics from your own life in order to chart a different course from the one you know. Awareness that grows out of the specifics of your own situation produces energy. For this reason, you need to know the details of your own experience in order to make some judgments about how to set a personal and professional direction for your life.

People who feel in charge automatically have a different energy level from those who plod along trying to survive from Monday through Friday. How well I remember the mental landscape I used to devise for my teaching week. I imagined that from Monday through Wednesday, I'd plod up a rising slope. I'd reach the mountain top late Wednesday afternoon, gaze ahead to the weekend, then begin my easy descent down the trail to the weekend's green pastures. Of course, my mental image rarely became a reality; my construct was my hazy self-construction of what I hoped my week might be like.

INVITATION: Maintain a one-week record of events in your life both in school and at home. Rate these events or incidents for: energy giving, energy taking, and a waste of time.

Invitations in this book allow you to carry out various assignments to give you more insight into the subject of human energy, yours and others. Most of the time, these exercises will apply directly to your life. I will do these assignments with you or show others who have tried them. It is important to maintain your journal or record keeping for at least a week. One or two days doesn't allow enough time to accommodate the ups and downs of a roller coaster week. The relationship between home and school may require even more time. One week of recordings may not be enough to give you the perspectives you need. Still, just recording and analyzing for one week will give you a mental framework to continue to think about the energy issue.

I asked six of the teacher participants in my study of energy to keep a weeklong diary in response to my main research question, "What gives you energy, takes it away, and for you is a waste of time?" They kept a detailed record of everything they did at home and at school for one complete week, including Saturday and Sunday. Each rated their entries with their best estimates of what took or gave energy and was a waste of time. They often stopped and gave lengthy written analyses for making their decisions. All of the participants had responsibilities at home. I included the weekends because no one ever "just teaches" and no one lives at home without responsibilities or is "just a parent." The two worlds of home and school intersect and need to be considered together and apart.

A Glimpse into Teachers' Lives

Each of the teachers used a slightly different approach to record and evaluate how he or she used time and interpreted the meaning of the evidence. I share these data now in preparation for your own examinations of your week. The first teacher, "Jack," a high-school English teacher, introduced a new category—neutral—in which he felt he could not get a reading on whether it took or gave energy. I share his record keeping, two days back-to-back: one for Sunday, and the other for Monday:

Code: AE: Add energy, TE: Take energy, N: neutral, WE: wastes energy.

Sunday: At Home
     9:00: Awaken, plans for the day. N
     9:15: Read paper and breakfast. N
     9:30: Read essays. N
     9:45: Further discussion about day. N
     9:50: Grade papers. N
    10:20: Errand in neighborhood: bank, shopping for food. N
    10:50: Pack, etc. to get out the door for day's adventure, make sandwiches. TE
    11:10: Neighbors show up with presents for boys, interruption prep for trip. TE

11:30: Eddie has meltdown in van (last 30 min; entirely about having to sit in back seat). TE

11:30: Drive to Eli's. TE

11:50: Drive to Point (45 min. drive in which Eddie continues to be difficult). TE

12:35: Picnic at Point—sunny, beautiful; had been gray and foggy. AE

12:55: Watch three boys play @ park while Sandy (wife) stays at picnic site with baby. AE

1:20: Sat with Sandy and talked about parenting/Littleton/evil while kids played @ playground. AE.

2:00: Walk along beach, through forest talking with Sandy with kids ahead of us looking for rocks and shells. AE
NOTE: This Point where we picnic is new to us and the new experience gives energy. AE

2:45: Stop at Point museum for snack after walk. N

2:55: Went through museum: interactive exhibits with kids. AE

3:55: Walk all the way back to retrieve van because kids too tired. AE

4:05: Wait outside museum with van while they finish museum. N

4:10: Drive home. N

4:30: Stop off in town where I teach for coffee and ice cream and I run into a student of mine. AE.

4:45: Drive home while Sandy and I talk some more. AE

6:00: Check e-mail, unpack from the day. N

6:30: Shower. AE
Dinner during which Sandy and I talk about summer plans and finances. AE

7:00: To playground with Walter to watch/help him practice riding his bike. AE

7:30: On to computer network to read, edit, post out to group. N

8:00: Sidetracked into a few different projects—when I should be doing schoolwork. TE

9:00: Schoolwork with intermittent time on NET. TE

Midnight: Back up work and close day with a few poems. N

Monday: School Day

5:50: Wake up to alarm and son asking for breakfast. When I say I'll get it he won't let me because he "wants mommy to get it." TE

6:00: Check e-mail before leaving. N

13

6:05:	Make lunch. N
6:10:	Stop by donut shop for coffee and donut I eat as I drive to work. N
6:15–6:55:	Drive to work during which time I listen to books on tape. N
6:55–8:00:	School before anyone else so I can copy, set up, be available to students. About 15 students meet in my room every morning to talk, work, hang out. AE
7:45:	Get mail, sample page layouts. AE
8:00:	Period 1: Work well, all prep pays off—competence energizes. AE
8:20:	Assumptions regarding work due is wrong. TE
10:05:	Former student comes by for advice. We talk for 15 min./being valued and helpful. AE
10:20:	Prep period, work on papers. TE
10:35:	Work interrupted by student with questions about his project after which I return to work. TE
10:50:	Go to copy exemplars from assignment I've been grading. Can't find them. WE
11:15–12:10:	Teaching fourth period. N
12:15–1:00:	Lunch alone reading *New Yorker*. N
1:05–2:05:	Junior class in library during which librarian drones on about how to use the library (TE) and my conferences with students. AE
2:05–3:00:	6th period. Jose (TE), conferences. AE
3:05:	Federico comes in for conference. TE
3:15:	Walk to office to check box before leaving. AE
3:20:	Humorous talk with colleague. AE
3:30:	Car won't start at first. TE
3:45:	Stop for snack for the drive. N
3:50–4:30:	Drive home. WE
4:30–4:45:	Check e-mail. N
4:45–6:30:	Nap, unusual to do this. AE
6:35:	Dinner with Sandy while we talk about $180 bill from plumber. TE
6:45:	Work with Sandy to help Eddie on homework assignment. N
7:00:	Go through mail, set up work for evening. N
7:30:	Take truck to mechanic for repair and walk eight blocks home. TE
	On way home see police officer and ask him to check on kid in neighborhood who may be dealing drugs or bringing trouble. AE

8:00:   Home to work on planning for tomorrow. TE
8:30:   Realize I left crucial papers (i.e., to help me with planning). TE
8:40–11:45:   Paperwork—student papers. TE/AE
11:45–12:00:   Tried to watch a former student's multimedia project but couldn't get it to download. WE.
12:05–12:45:   Done with work I read a few poems & Pinsky's *Sounds of Poetry* because I am challenging self, learning. AE
12:45:   To bed.

Jack then reviewed his recordings for the week then reflected on the meaning of what he had seen. Jack liked what he saw, though he was objective about the many mundane things that filled his life:

I found myself thinking often about the story of Sysiphus from Carnus, about how everyone has to push the rock up the mountain (thus taking energy) and it is only in the shadow of that pushing, in the hours it takes for him to walk down the mountain, in the lull of the work he must do, that he gets to think about what he wants to. So much of the week I charted my life seemed divided into those moments when I did what I *had* to do versus what I *wanted* or even *needed* to do. In short, I felt achievements—as a reader, husband, father, teacher, human—gave me energy, demands, especially from those whose tradition is to take.

Certain people I find I associate with energy—i.e., I have come to expect they will fuel me, somehow feed me: Jerry, my colleague with whom I discuss poetry almost daily; we allow each other the power of an identify other than the teacher we both know we are: to each other we give permission to be the poets we both also call ourselves. My wife, sometimes from just from being with her, others from talking with her, still others from just thinking about her, she completes me, guides me, accompanies me, I have no equivalent friend nor any other who can fill me so full so fast. My editor, whose confidence in me, inspires in me a belief in myself that could power a car for the energy she summons. My students, past and present, the NET, my personal online community which exists through me, a responsibility and creation that prides me through my days despite its rather mundane demands.

While I am trying to be precise in my notes there are certain habits and rituals I cannot capture in such minutia:

15

- Constantly punctuating most activities in any setting with notes on 3 x 5 cards for books and articles.
- While waiting anywhere for more than a minute or two I might take out my Palm Pilot and sort through to dos, make notes, read from the book or magazine I carry with me (usually poetry).
- While working in office, take intermittent breaks from work to: cleans palate with a poem; listen to music, jot ideas for chapters and projects on the whiteboards in the office; back away from work to just "think" for a few minutes; miscellaneous maintenance activities within the office; check e-mail on the NET; check my Web site to see if the student who manages it has incorporated the changes I suggested.

After surveying the minutia of his recordings, Jack steps back to consider the nature of his life. He feels in control and is happy with the balance of his life. He knows there are some positive elements in his life that he wishes he could increase. I'm sure there are days when he wishes he could do nothing but read and write poetry. Nevertheless, as a father/husband/teacher/writer, he knows there are responsibilities he needs and wants to maintain. He is pleased that he has turned energy-taking events into energy-giving events. I refer to the squalling in the car enroute to a family picnic that was turned into an energy giver on arrival at the park on Sunday.

He is also aware that he maintains a constant intellectual challenge through his 3 x 5 cards, the reading of poetry, writing on notes on the dashboard of his car, or listening to books on tape while driving to work. Jack has high focus about the direction of his life and therefore knows better how he will maintain a constant high-energy climate as well as how to turn normally negative forces into positive ones. He has a strong relationship with Jerry, his teaching colleague and poet. I am reminded that if there is enough depth to a community of two, it supplies enough professional energy for both. Too many times people lament that their school or department gives them little professional energy. But, the data in this study show that one significant relationship is enough to sustain anyone professionally.

My next participant, "Louise," is a second-grade teacher with a small family. Her approach to recording the week's events are different in that she stops at the end of each day to write a narrative about what gives her energy, takes it away, and is a waste of time. You may wish to consider this approach. She also includes family life in the energy equation. She is writing in April, toward the end of her school year:

Wednesday: Well, there are more things on my energy-taker list today. This time of year is always exhausting at school. It is the time when transfers happen, when new positions are posted, when administrators are moved, etc. So, the rumors are constant. As teachers, it seems like we always just wait to see where we are placed. The district is also growing and students are being moved to various elementary schools. Parents are in an uproar. I think I am pretty good at looking at the whole picture, but this time of year is stressful for everyone.

I got an e-mail from a friend who teaches intermediate level in another building in the district. She is transferring buildings and grade levels because she does not want to deal with the state testing any more. She said that she cannot continue to compromise what she knows and believes because of these tests. She is a very dedicated teacher and it worries me that she is burning out a bit. She realizes that playing this game for so long is really wearing on you. So, she has made a personal decision to get out of a stressful situation. My worry is that all of our strong intermediate teachers are leaving intermediate for similar reasons.

We also had a meeting with the superintendent today. Again, it feels like teachers are the last to know what is happening to our staff and our students. We were also told by a committee that we would be going back to textbooks for all K–5 students in social studies. These are the things that take my energy and it seems like today they were nonstop. This is typical for this time of year, I remember, but it is exhausting to see so many decisions made without the best interests of kids in mind.

This gives the flavor of her drainers. She continued to discuss others:

Necessary precaution procedures because of the Columbine shooting incident

Parent in another town suing the school because her child is not on grade level

Louise is married with a child in elementary school. She finds that, whereas school is an energy taker, on this particular day, the opposite is the case at home.

The evening was full of energy givers. My daughter is taking piano lessons and was given a homework assignment to study flash cards. She realized that she loved flash cards in other things. She wanted more. She was dancing and happy—really loving these things.

Louise has made several observations about home life in relation to her teaching:

- Dinner with family is relaxing
- Exercise and chatting with friends is relaxing
- Interests not directly related to school
- Service projects
- Working on a very important professional award, support of friends

Louise sums up a general sense of her energy sources: "I think that I am noticing that I have many interests that are related to teaching but not actually teaching. I think that most of the energy comes from other people who think like I do or who challenge me to think beyond my current beliefs." Louise's statement is one that was repeated by every one of the study participants: People give energy, and they take it away.

INVITATION: *Do a first reading of your weekly recordings and postings. What is your impression? What surprised you?*

You will explore this exercise after you have posted your ratings of what gives, takes energy and is a waste of time. You may wish to consider a number of approaches to your reading:

1. Reread each of the categories separately, for example, "Takes energy" or "Gives energy."
2. Reread to examine the relationship between home and school energy. Are they connected?

INVITATION: *Were there specific people who gave you energy? Took it away?*

This invitation should give you more insight into what gives and takes energy. Consider all the immediate people from students to administrators, parents, family members, or friends and your relationships with them.

INVITATION: Consider distant events that may not affect you in the immediate sense but still may contribute to your energy level.

Recall Louise's reflection about the shifts in faculty members and the shuffling of assignments that cause unrest. Louise was also concerned about a colleague who asked for a change of position because of the effect of testing. You could almost feel the activation of early warning systems with this incident and the items following: suing of the school by a parent whose child was not up to grade level. School bond issues, letters to the editor about schools, both supportive and nonsupportive, may distantly affect energy levels.

INVITATION: Rethink your data or lesson plans for what constitutes a waste of time.

Both of my participants in this chapter seldom referred to this category. In fairness, I did not challenge them to step farther back from their recordings to take a deeper look. Consider this in relation to the following questions:

1. Are there policies, materials, expectations, or conditions that cause me to waste my students' time?
2. What curricula am I teaching that I know will not benefit my students?
3. At what points in my teaching am I covering material instead of teaching it?
4. What aspects of my teaching will not contribute effectively to my students, long-term view of learning?

When we waste our students' time, we often feel an energy drain that is more subconscious than is immediately apparent. I find that teachers can experience much drain when they instinctively know that certain practices are not contributing to long-term learning. For example, time spent covering material that may appear on a mandated state test may help them boost scores but may not result in significant long-term learning.

Reflection

You have recorded data about your week, both at home and in school, in order to sense the sources of what gives you energy and what may contribute to drain. The invitations you engaged in should sensitize you to the specific issues and people who have an effect on your energy supply. People are often our greatest source of energy as well as the most significant contributors to drain.

What constitutes a waste of time is more difficult to assess. We are only beginning to investigate the territory in the last invitaton. This step requires a long step back from what we busily do each day.

3

Setting a Clear Direction

You have completed your analysis of a week of personal and professional activity. You want to increase what gives you energy and decrease what takes it away. Perhaps you, like many others, have realized that what drains energy most is when your professional options are reduced, or when decisions are made for you, and you can only react to events instead of shaping them.

One of the greatest energy-giving factors is having a clear sense of personal and professional direction. In short, you need to know what you say "yes" to in order to take control of your life. You want to be proactive and move actively to change and affect what is around you. This chapter offers a series of invitations that will help you to state more clearly what you want to affirm. The first set of invitations will focus on your teaching/learning history. The next set will focus on the students you teach. Finally, you will decide what you need to learn in order to be the professional you envision.

I look back over my personal and professional life and view a career of much-wasted energy. Much of the waste was due to ignorance and a lack of maturity. What kept me on the upward spiral seemed to be a fundamental pragmatism, "What works for learning and living?" Other simple questions, "What's fair? What's just?" tempered the pragmatism. The first day I taught school our second daughter, Alyce, was born and within five years our family grew to four children. I had no real direction or objective other than to survive my teaching, and not long after, being a principal. I worked hard to provide for our growing family. I worked summers and also completed a master's degree in the same time frame. Although I made some choices, most of my living could be characterized as reactive, doing what others asked of me, whether it was the job or family responsibilities. I experienced the full emotional roller coaster that accompanies teaching and administrative duties.

I was raised to believe that hard work solved any problem. I therefore simply put my head down and worked through one crisis after another. I rarely looked up to see where my directions were taking me. In fact, I had no direction. My compass direction read, "survive and provide."

If you want to save energy and have a clearer sense of direction, Steven Covey (1989) says, "Start with the end in mind." By the end of this chapter I anticipate you will be able to write a brief statement of the goals that will be the end you have in mind.

Examine What You Do Well

INVITATION: *Begin the direction-setting process by examining what you do well professionally.*

Forget about modesty. Begin a list, however short, and add to it over the next week. You ask, "What do you mean, do well?" I don't mean well in relation to other teachers. I mean of all the things you do, which ones are better than others? I go back to my first year of teaching and make a short list of what I remember as being positive elements in my profile:

- Reads aloud well
- Has a sense of drama
- Engenders interest in a new subject
- Has a sense of humor
- Speaks easily with most parents
- Is curious about new things—professionally, intellectually
- Tells stories

If at that time I had written a list of what I *couldn't* do or where I felt inept, the list would have been far longer. Another way to approach this invitation is to ask the question, "What do I enjoy most about teaching?" Usually, your competency comes at the point of what you genuinely enjoy doing. Examining the above list, your judgment would be correct if you said, "Graves enjoys performing or being in front of an audience." I taught because I enjoyed sharing things with an audience.

22

One of the wonderful things about teaching is that just about anything you enjoy or have done can apply to helping others learn. If you enjoy crafts, sewing, building, nature, growing flowers, singing, or playing an instrument, these skills can help you teach. Think back to when you showed another person how to do something—a younger brother or sister, a new person on a summer job, or coaching a sport.

INVITATION: *Think of anything you know how to do and try to recapture the event of learning itself.*

As much as we need to know what we teach well, we also need to know how we learn. You've been both a spectator and participant in learning all your life. Before I wrote *How to Catch a Shark and Other Stories About Teaching and Learning* (1998) I had no idea how many learning events had been part of my life. I began by listing anything I knew how to do: tie my shoe, drive a car, throw a baseball, shave, brush my teeth, or hit a golf ball. Next I tried to remember who taught me each skill and finally the actual process of being taught. Naturally, my parents were very important teachers in my life. Make a list of these learning events to get a sense of how you learn. Of course, some important teachers from school and university will emerge, as well as informal teachers from home, the neighborhood, sports teams, and the like.

INVITATION: *List the teachers you have had both in school and out, who have had influence on both your learning and teaching.*

In the first chapter of *A Fresh Look at Writing* (1994), I went back and listed all the teachers I could recall by name both in school and out. I listed these teachers because I knew that the professional I wanted to become would probably be constructed partly by important people from my past. Figure 3–1 shows these important people. Notice that I included negative teachers (not their real names) because there were certain people I did not want to emulate.

I acquired my skills in a variety of ways. Ms. Jones was encouraging and enthusiastic: She liked the way I read aloud and I've enjoyed reading aloud ever since. Several teachers were systematic and demanding, as in the case of Miss Johnson and Miss Valente, my mathematics and Latin teachers. I did rather poorly by school standards, only receiving

	TEACHERS IN SCHOOL	TEACHERS OUT OF SCHOOL
PRIMARY	ms. Jones SK	mom Dad
INTERMEDIATE	ms. adams K	mom Dad
JUNIOR HIGH	ms. Johnson S	Grandpa Hiller mom
SENIOR HIGH	ms. Dower S+ ms. ditch K+ mr. muller SK+ ms. Valente S ms. mclinus S mr. motyl S mr. Black N mr. Rogers N	mom H Nelson Wilbur Grandpa Hiller
COLLEGE	Prof. Berkleman S Prof. Seward SK Prof. Fairfield K Prof. Rangely N	mom Tip Weeks H. Nelson Wilbur
POST COLLEGE	D. Durrell SK J. Fiore SK M. Barth SK A. Roden K	Cdr. Stepanoff Lt. Raleigh Dr. Burack L. Cohen G. Demarest E. Padginton H Porter D. murray m.E Giacobve L. Funkhouser

S: Learn a skill   N: Negative Teachers
K: Teacher making personal connections

Figure 3–1. Teacher memory exercise

C's in each, but I am aware that I still remember most of my Latin today even though I only had a year of it fifty-four years ago.

Mr. Muller taught me skills while I had fun. Each week we'd sing in Spanish, and I still carry some Spanish with me because of my enjoyment of the singing. He also immersed us in the language by speaking only Spanish in class, and he remains an important figure in my teaching today. Learning a subject by immersion from someone who knows and enjoys it is a key factor in my teaching approach and philosophy. All of these teachers expected more of me and we had a strong enough personal connection that I did not want to disappoint them.

Understand Your Students

I had very little experience to draw on when I began teaching my class of thirty-nine sixth and seventh graders in 1956. There was a desperate need for teachers in those days so I began teaching after taking an intensive eight-week teacher preparation course for college graduates in any field. I took the course the day after I was mustered out of four years in the U. S. Coast Guard. The only teaching I had done was on Sunday morning in our church in Boston, a few short lessons in the intensive teacher preparation course, and one small workshop in the service. In retrospect, the one thing I'd learned in each of those brief teaching situations was to get to know the student at a personal level. I seemed to know how to get to know someone quickly and remember the details of the encounter for the sake of the student's learning. I don't know how that is learned but it did help me to survive my first years of teaching.

If I wish to set a clear direction professionally, then I need to include some understanding of my students. To sense how you will include students in your end statement, there are number of invitations to guide you.

INVITATION: *Gain an impression of your class through a three-column exercise in which you first list students' names from memory in one column, list specific things that each student knows in the next column, and check the third column when the student knows that you know they know that.*

First Memory Attempt

	Experiences and Interests	*Confirmation Column*
1. Fred Gallo	Sharks	
2. Marcella Cowan	Horses	X
3. John Pringle		
4. Allison Goodrich		
5. Norman Frazier	Sister in hospital	X
6. Delores Sunderland	Sea life, birds	
7. Frances Sawtelle		
8. Johnathan Freedman	Prehistoric animals	
9. Charles Lentini	Motorcycles	
10. Aleka Alphanosopoulos	Singing	
11. Jason Beckwith		
12. Jon Finlayson		**
13. Joel Cupperman		
14. Mark Andrade		
15. Patricia Rezendes		
16. Betty Oliver		
17. Margaret Texeira		
18. Marcus Washington		
19. Patricia Snow		
20. William Frost		
21. Paul Gardner		
22. Jason Tompkins		
23. Ford Park		
24. Laurie Kunstler		
25. Albert Guimond		

** All children below the line were not remembered on first attempt on the second day of school.

Figure 3–2a. First memory attempt

Since students are one of our most important energy sources, we need to consider how they affect us. Further, they need to be included in our statement of goals at the end of this chapter.

INVITATION: *Number from 1 to 25 in the first column. Next, write all the names of the children opposite those numbers. (In my first attempt, I could only remember twelve from memory.) See Figure 3–2b. Then fill*

Second Memory Attempt

	Experiences and Interests	Confirmation Column
1. Marcella Cowan	Horses, birth of foal	X
2. Norman Frazier	Sister well, fishing	X
3. Johnathan Freedman	Tyrannasaurus rex, brontosaurus, draws well	X
4. Marcus Washington	Athlete, kick ball	
5. Delores Sunderland	Any craft, especially painting, sea life	X
6. Jon Finlayson	Football, collects cards of athletes	X
7. Betty Oliver	Takes care of little sister, cooks	X
8. John Pringle		
9. Frances Sawtelle	Cat and kittens	
10. Ford Park	Works with father on road-moving equipment on Saturdays	X
11. Joel Cupperman		
12. Jason Beckwith		
13. Fred Gallo	Sharks, movie "Jaws"	
14. Aleka Alphanosopoulos	Collects records	X
15. Charles Lentini	Collects motorcycle brochures, brother has cycle	
16. Allison Goodrich		
17. Mark Andrade	Fishes with father	
18. Jason Tompkins		
19. Paul Gardner	Traveled to dog show	
20. Margaret Texeira	Cares for little brother and sister, this angers her	X

_____ ***

21. Albert Guimond		
22. Patricia Snow		
23. Patricia Rezendes	Knows something about weaving	
24. William Frost		
25. Laurie Kunstler		

*** All children below the line were not remembered on second attempt one week after school started.

Figure 3–2b. Second memory attempt

in details about content ability, process data (knows how to), or physical and artistic skills in the middle column. Place a check in the first column if you have confirmed that the child knows the information or skill.

For example, in Figure 3–2, I remembered Marcella Cowan's name, that she was interested in horses, and was able to confirm that interest for her. Confirmation must be as specific as possible as in the following types:

- "Marcella, I see you must be interested in horses. *Black Beauty* is your third book on horses. Do I have that right? Can you tell me more about that?"
- "Marcella, I overheard that you actually have a horse on your farm and that you care for it. Do I have that right? Can you tell me more about that?"
- (After reading her short paper) "Marcella, do I have this right? You actually got a blue ribbon for your horse, Beauty? Can you tell me more about that?"

Naturally, I am interested in the child's reaction to the confirmation. Usually, confirmation for the child means even more information when I ask, "Can you tell me more about that?" My ultimate objective is to carry all children in memory, know their specific abilities and interests, and have confirmed for each child a beginning point for the two of us to begin to learn together. To work through this invitation, I suggest you try to do the memory work twice and about three days apart to note progress. At this point, consider some of the following questions for reflection about your future statement at the end of this chapter. I'll answer these questions for myself from the exercise:

- Do you remember boys more easily than girls? *Out of twelve children, I remembered seven boys.*
- Speculate on why some children's names come to you more quickly than others. *(The children call more attention to themselves with what they know, or by strong personality.)*
- Speculate on why (after the second memory attempt at names) some children's names are more difficult to remember. *(These children do not want to be noticed, are usually quieter, or have problems with learning.)*

28

- Did you notice a spark of energy for you and the child at the point of confirming the knowledge in column 3? (*I had many more details after the second attempt and therefore got more reaction. This is definitely an energy giver for the student and myself.*)

INVITATION: *Observe six of your students in at least two other settings than the classroom.*

I especially want to observe children who slip from my memory (as in Albert, the two Patricias, William, and Laurie). I want to observe them on the playground, in art class, or physical education, or their social behavior with others. I want to move away from the more dominant way of knowing children through spoken words and written words, and catch other abilities and impressions. I also find it useful to try to look at the world through their eyes. I try to become that child. How does she regard the behavior of others? What causes him to focus his attentions?

Working Toward the End Statement

INVITATION: *What do you wish to know more about?*

Setting a clear direction to a specific destination as a professional, I know there are certain things I need to know more about. For any kind of energy return in the future, I have to be in the process of focused learning. Usually, I want to extend what I already know and consider some areas of knowledge I just can't do without. I may even ask some of my former mentors this question: "If I want to be more proficient at X, what do I need to know?"

Consider two approaches to this invitation. First, look at the areas in which you are confident in what you know. What would you do to increase that knowledge and ability? Second, as you look at essential areas that will be of particular help to your students, what skills do you need? For example, at the end of my first year of teaching I needed to know more about the teaching of reading. Indeed, the need was apparent the second day I taught. The need grew throughout the year, and has not ended to this day. You may wish to acquire skills in other curriculum areas such as math, science, writing, or the arts.

29

INVITATION: Formulate the end statement toward which you will be working the next five years.

In each of the invitations in this chapter, you have been cultivating the ground that will help you to formulate an end statement about where you wish to be at the end of the next five years. Begin by making a *vocational statement* along the lines of some of the following statements:

A. I wish to become a team leader for our primary unit.
B. I wish to change greatly as a middle-school teacher and ultimately make presentations at our regional IRA conferences.
C. I wish to complete my degree in administration and become an assistant principal.
D. I wish to be chair of the English department in our high school.

Part of an end statement includes a *learning statement.* Learning statements are made up of extending what you enjoy doing well. Since students are a part of everything we do in education, learning statements also include how we learn from them and about them. You may also wish to include a curriculum statement as part of learning on the way to your objective. I will build on each of the different types of vocational statements (A–D above) to show various learning statements:

A. I wish to become team leader for our primary unit. I enjoy being organized and I want to take this skill and introduce a portfolio program in our unit. But I need to investigate how others have worked with it, read, and stay in close touch with my students' interpretations of how this approach is working. I'll try several approaches and learn from those. Some students won't handle them well and I need to adjust to learn how that can work. I'll begin with a language portfolio.

B. I wish to change greatly as a middle-school teacher and ultimately make presentations at our regional IRA conferences. I love coaching our drama club and presenting two plays a year. I want to learn how to integrate drama into the full curriculum. Drama has everything from content to process, to end product. I know there needs to be many entry points for all kinds of students if this is to work. That's going to take five years! I need to draw on my mentors from university. I'll take social studies to show how this can be done. This is precisely what I want to present at regional IRA. I present well but I've lacked the real content to do this.

C. I wish to complete my degree in administration and become an assistant principal. I think I'm pretty good at working with people, especially staff and kids. I know I need to know more about evaluation, especially standards, if I aim to be an assistant principal. I need to know more about how kids view evaluation; they need, along with staff, to take greater interest in it. So, I need to see what works, and the best way to do it. I'll experiment now so I'll have more answers.

D. I wish to be chair of the English department in our high school. I've had A. P. English for three years and I know I teach it well, especially the writing on which they consistently score well. As chair I'd need to look toward including all kids. I need to take on some of the freshman English sections to learn how that's done. What I learn there I need to figure a way to do workshops with other teachers. I've got to read and see some experts doing it well. Kids must have views about this. Got to ask them what works, doesn't work for them.

The last part of your statement includes a section on mentors and monitoring. You'll want to include the best of mentors to help you realize your end statement. You already have some understanding of what types of teachers or mentors have helped you in the past. You won't want to neglect the energy that comes from consistent contact and exploration from someone who has gone on before you. You know the mentor is the type of person who will be a good guide for the way you learn best. If you can't find a mentor type sometimes a colleague with whom you work especially well can at least listen and react to what you have chosen to do.

You also need a brief statement about how you will monitor progress toward realizing your objective. Some people keep a journal and write frank statements about progress or lack of it, or report how their mentor or colleague is helping them. Others keep portfolios with materials, short written reflections, and good articles. Both approaches are specific in reporting the progress of their students (or lack of it) in relation to their end statement. The final four statements with the addition of mentors and monitoring in italic now read as follows:

A. I wish to become team leader for our primary unit. I enjoy being organized and I want to take this skill and introduce a portfolio program in our unit. But I need to investigate how others have worked

31

with it, read, and stay in close touch with my students' interpretation of how this approach is working. I'll try several approaches and learn from those. Some students won't handle them well and I need to adjust how to learn how that can work. I'll begin with a language portfolio. *I'm in touch with Jennie Trimble in another unit and building in our system. She's done it for several years now and gets along well. I think she'd take me on. As for keeping in touch with my progress, it seems logical to keep my own portfolio and learn along with my students.*

B. I wish to change greatly as a middle-school teacher and ultimately make presentations at our regional IRA conferences. I love coaching our drama club and presenting two plays a year. I want to learn how to integrate drama into the full curriculum. Drama has everything from content to process, to end product. I know there need to be many entry points for all kinds of students if this is to work. That's going to take five years! I need to draw on my mentors from university. I'll take social studies to show how this can be done. This is precisely what I want to present at regional IRA. I present well but I've lacked the real content to do this. *I guess I could go on e-mail with Professor Magnuson at university if he's willing. I think he might be interested in this for his own learning. I lean toward a collection of videos to keep track along with my own portfolio, plus e-mails that I'll print out.*

C. I wish to complete my degree in administration and become an assistant principal. I think I'm pretty good at working with people, especially staff and kids. I know I need to know more about evaluation, especially standards, if I aim to be an assistant principal. I need to know more about how kids view evaluation; they need, along with staff, to take greater interest in it. So, I need to see what works, and the best way to do it. I'll experiment now so I'll have more answers. *I've heard that Professor Barbero knows assessment very well and is on the state standards committee. Maybe she'd take me on for independent study. I'll write a paper for the study but I'm not much for keeping journals or portfolios. I'll come up with something.*

D. I wish to be chair of the English department in our high school. I've had A. P. English for three years and I know I teach it well, especially the writing on which they consistently score well. As chair I know I'd have to reach more kids. I need to take some of the freshman English sections to learn how that's done. What I learn there I need to figure a way to do workshops with other teachers. I've got to read and see some experts doing it well. Kids must have views about this. Got to ask them what works, doesn't work for them on the writing. *East High across town has a crackerjack chair, Dr. Kenniston. Their whole school has taken state honors. Maybe I could get into their department, or at the least interview him and see if he'd mentor me.*

Reflection

You have carefully reviewed your teaching and what you enjoy within the profession. Further, you've looked back at your own school career and ways in which you learned in school and out. You have a sense of how you best learn as well as what you enjoy teaching. You experimented with the three-column exercise to examine carefully your relationship to your students. Then you looked ahead to writing an end statement about where you wish you'd be at the end of five years.

An essential part of reaching an objective, as well as experiencing the energy that accompanies the journey, is to specify what you want to learn. Some of the learning comes from your students, colleagues, and especially from mentors you have asked to help you.

4

Structure the Class for the Release of Student Energy

I easily recall my first week teaching sixth and seventh grade. I stood before the class waving my arms in excitement about our new detective club during reading class. I'd give a few clues about a text and everyone raced to find the passage in the text that matched the clue. The principal and reading supervisor were quite impressed when they observed my lesson. I was impressed that they were impressed. The reading supervisor asked, "Don, what will you do as a follow-up?"

I hadn't the slightest idea what I would do. My planning was a day-by-day affair. Each night I'd go home and construct one lesson for the next day. I knew something about motivation and seemed to have the ability to get students enthused. Unfortunately, my motivators were not connected to any long-term plan. Worse, the motivators all depended on me. My translation of the meaning of motivation was, "Put on a show that triggers students into enthusiastic learning."

The students' energy had little root in themselves. I'm often asked in my workshops around the country, "How do I *get* students to write?" The question is usually asking for some quick motivators that will inspire children to write. Unfortunately, they don't exist. Teachers who ask these questions will soon find themselves in my predicament during my first year of teaching. Each generation of children has become more sophisticated regarding matters of motivation. Children witness hundreds of commercials produced by experts with million-dollar budgets each week. They are well versed in reading external stimulants to move their desires and opinions.

The Classroom Environment

What educates and releases significant energy in students is not methodologies but carefully orchestrated classroom conditions. I think

34

the use of course descriptions titled, "Methods in the Teaching of Reading" or "Methods in the Teaching of Mathematics," are throwbacks to an age when motivators and stimulants were the vogue in teaching. Of course, these same approaches are around and publishers still claim their books contain the best method. The method approach suggests that learning can be broken up into tiny bits of skill and information. The classroom environment becomes secondary to the method. As teachers, we make up a major part of the environment.

The conditions for learning set by my mother at home contributed more to my education than any other single factor in my life. The conditions she set were an insatiable curiosity about learning through the books she read. She carefully arranged visits, trips, and toys. She asked more questions of herself and therefore allowed us to see where she was headed in her next learning project. She delighted in the questions my brother and I asked of her. Occasionally, she would show us how to do something and punctuate the demonstration with short sermons tinged with the morality of living and the right way to do things.

It is the quality of our own lives as we engage with the world that is one of the major sources of energy for our students. It is the questions you ask aloud about the world, your curiosity, the books you read, and your personal use of writing that teach far more than any methodological course you've ever taken. Yes, there are approaches to teaching that we need to know but they take second place to the conditions for learning. You, the teacher, are the most important condition in the room.

INVITATION: Structure the room for joint action and responsibility.

Children bring an abundance of energy to the classroom. Unless there are specific limits midst a wide range of choice, the energy will be diffused in wasteful ways. Children come from such a variety of homes, each having its own set of limits, that it is not surprising that the meaning of a spoken limit has to be tested. Some homes are autocratic and the children may have very little choice. Others are quite permissive with no set time for meals or bed. The children have few household responsibilities. Children from both types of families enter your room and both have to learn what your limits mean. Children want to know how secure their environment is if they are to function in it.

Every material and area in the room has a range and a limit. Most of all, each has a function for learning that requires explanation. But explanation is not enough. The explanation must be accompanied by demonstration: "And over here, we have several racks of books. The green sticker means that for most of you it is an easy book, the blue a sort of middle book, and the red is a challenge book. Timmy, would you go and pick out an easy book that you'd like to read and bring it over here. Okay, you've done that. Now when you finish, put it back where you got it from. Show me how you'd do that. Okay, class, why are these books put together in this manner?"

Every class has its own needs for limit setting. Part of living in a community and benefiting from the energy a community has to offer is learning the functions of all the various items and the limits to which things can be used, so that maximal choice can be exercised without teacher supervision. Choice, of course, is often misunderstood by children who have no choices allowed at home. They will often "overshoot" in their interpretation of the options you have given them. That is, their unspoken interpretation may be, "Here is a generous teacher. I think I'll take a little more. She'll understand."

INVITATION: *Check the effectiveness of the classroom understructure.*

For this invitation, you may wish to explore the effectiveness of one area or the entire classroom. If I choose one area or section of the room, then I take several children and ask these types of questions:

- Tell me how this works. Show me how this works.
- What can you do with these things?
- What do you use them for?
- What do we have these things for?
- Suppose you run into this problem here, how would you handle it?
- How does it work if someone else is here too?
- Tell me all the different things you can do with this.

Above all, I want to learn if children can be specific about the function of the area, how problems are solved in it, and their sense of option with the materials. On some occasions I may ask the children after my preliminary questions, "Tell me, how can this area work better than it does now? What's not working? What is working?"

Building Community
INVITATION: If you have not tried the three-column memory exercise in Chapter 3 be sure to try it now.

The last time you tried this exercise you were checking your vocational sensitivity to children. This time you are deliberately setting out to give each person a "knowing" place within the classroom community. I absolutely must look at each child's face as I know they know something special. I must know this with specificity. For children who struggle, I need to know with even greater detail what they know. Further, I want to confirm that knowing in the presence of other children. I am most satisfied when my continual reiteration of what children know is picked up by other children who deliberately make the same confirmations. Confirmation of a knowledge or knowing how to do something by other children is the ultimate building of community and the source of great energy for learning.

INVITATION: When children are accurate, ask them how they managed to do it correctly.

I continually sprinkle the class with these kinds of observations. When a period is in the right place, a math problem has been solved, a child has done a particularly good job cleaning an area, or the class has worked especially well, I simply say, "That's just right; this is marvelous, how did you figure how to do that?" Children enjoy trying to rediscover the process of something that has worked especially well. We both gain energy in this kind of inquiry.

So much of structuring a classroom for higher energy involves listening to children and finding out what they think about the classroom, their books, writing, math problems, and special interests. I need all this information to redefine limits with the children and to channel their energies effectively.

Sharing Responsibilities
INVITATION: What responsibilities are you assuming that the children ought to be able to do for themselves?

37

When you and your students take joint responsibility for the effective operation of the classroom, there is energy in the feeling of community that accompanies that accomplishment. Room cleanliness, the orderliness of books, libraries, folders, and displays can be handled by the children. Further, I know of teachers who have children who help in scheduling conferences, writing letters of invitation, thank-you letters, even assisting in conferences about writing, math, and so forth. Of course, these responsibilities take careful teaching and development. When responsibilities are rotated, the former helper teaches the new person about the job.

In some buildings, grade-level meetings are held in which discussions center around what responsibilities have been assumed in the various rooms. In some cases, responsibilities have been assumed that others had never conceived of being handled by the children. "You mean, you allow children to do that? You mean they really can?"

I know of another teacher who began the school year with desks, chairs, artwork, displays, supplies, and tables all in a heap in the center of the room. The stunned children found the teacher sitting on a rug in a corner of the room. He waved them over to sit around him. "Now," he said, "We're going to make this room ours. We're going to come up with new ideas about how a room should be arranged; we'll discuss our studies and what we want to learn together." He was a highly skilled teacher and knew just how to involve the children from the start. I confess that I've never had the courage to try his approach. On the other hand when I have the entire room set just the way I want it, with all artwork and books displayed to my satisfaction, I can hardly call the room "our" place in which to live and work.

For this next invitation, consider taking one or two responsibilities that several strong students should be able to handle. Remember to carefully teach the children how to assume the task. Teaching means showing them how.

INVITATION: *Evaluate your accommodation for all-class performances within the classroom.*

All-class performances include every child simultaneously. I find that great energy is developed when there are performance items in my informal classroom curriculum. I specifically mention choral speaking, or choral reading aloud, informal drama, even pantomime expression through drama. I find that children or students of any age can learn quickly to do choral speaking. You will find help with the process of choral speaking in *Explore Poetry* (Graves, 1992). I find that children as young as six and seven can learn several poems in a week's time. Best of all, the class has a sense of "we can do these things." Music is a natural area for children to feel group energy. If you enjoy singing or playing a musical instrument, enjoy this time together.

All-class approaches to class performance are particularly helpful to children who feel separated from the class or who struggle with a world filled with an emphasis on written words.

INVITATION: *Take on an energy-giving project that involves the entire classroom looking beyond itself to help others.*

We live in self-centered times. I witness this atmosphere playing itself in my own classroom when a child responds to my query, "Timmy, why did you take Roger's library book?" Timmy responds, "I wanted it." He obviously feels his answer is sufficient for my understanding. Timmy's answer tells me that I have much work to do to help Timmy understand another's point of view.

"I certainly understand that you want it. Tell me, you are now Roger; how is he feeling now that this book he's been reading has been taken from him?" Timmy is puzzled by my question and strains to shift to another point of view. There will be many such exchanges throughout the year and between other children in the classroom.

I've found there is energy in preparing to help others. First, it usually gives everyone an opportunity to contribute. Second, it shifts the focus of the class from self to others. This gives the class a sense of its own power: "We can do these things." Third, witnessing the effect of service with others is freeing to children. Finally, it is quite energy giving to you the teacher, to witness your class transcending their own individual needs. Their power becomes your energy-giving power.

As much as possible, choose a project beyond the school but immediate enough in geography for the children to see the faces of those they may assist. There are many different kinds of projects to consider.

I especially mention nursing homes and senior day centers. People in these locations are cut off from children and young people. Choral speaking and singing are fine offerings. If the children bring small personal articles such as photos, CDs, or models with them they often help communication. I will often do workshops to help the children. Consider also day care centers and private kindergartens who always welcome visits from older students. There may be some of these centers within walking distance of your school.

Encouraging Discovery
INVITATION: Assess the Discovery Quotient in Your Classrom

David McCullough, the famous historian, in a recent interview with Roger Mudd on the History Channel, spoke about his teaching of history at Cornell University. He says, "I'm not satisfied until my students fall in love with history."

"How do you accomplish that?" asks Mudd.

"The key is to set things up so they discover history." McCullogh went on to say he chooses artifacts from a particular time period. The students received artifacts—a book, a blueprint, a musical score, a photo or a painting. They were to discover the time period through those artifacts. Those objects eventually led to people and it was through the eyes of those people that the time period was understood. "If students discovered history they'd learn to love it. McCullough's point could be applied to any subject area in the curriculum. Of course, we need to know our curriculum areas well enough to choose wisely. Children need to work with the stuff of science: observe and record. Clearly, there is energy in this kind of discovery. As teachers we need to travel with them to learn the disciplines that lead to actual discovery. We travel through nature observing the stuff of science. We solve real-life mathematical problems and learn how math can contribute to daily living.

Your task in this invitation is to examine a curriculum area and decide what part is open for children to discover and observe anew without having preset expectations. For example, I recall Nancie Atwell, a middle-school teacher, who gave the books she hadn't necessarily read to some struggling students asking them, "I'd really like to know your opinion about this because I haven't had time to read it yet." She was deliberately setting her students up for discovery. When students know that we have read a book ten times and we ask for their opinion, it makes discovery a little more difficult.

INVITATION: Take ten minutes, five days in a row to move about the room deliberately questioning and observing your students. Listen to their responses.

This is simply a more active exercise in learning more about what your students know. You will disengage from correcting, extending, showing, or advising as you move about the room while the children are working in reading, writing, science, or any other aspect of curriculum. You have given them an assignment to work steadily for the next twenty minutes. The following are some examples of learning by listening:

- *Reading:* "Tell me what is happening here"—pointing to story or book. Or, "What's the book about?" "So, this is about a girl who . . ."
- *Writing:* I deliberately look for something that is accurate, ignoring all other errors. "I see you have this capital just right here. How did you know how to do that? How did you figure that out?"
- *Science:* "I see you've found a book on X. Tell me about that. How did you happen to choose it?"
- *Math:* "I see that you've done two steps to this problem already. How did you figure it out? Tell me from the beginning."

You may feel the pressure to teach more actively. We all feel the preciousness of time in our busy days. In carrying out this invitation you are teaching, but in a very different way. You are helping your students to discover what they know. Indeed, you are helping yourself to know how they conceptualize their learning. You are helping them to articulate learning stories and to let them know they are learners. If a child has done something accurately it does not necessarily mean he or she can step back and explain how it was accomplished. Try to notice the countenance of the child when you point out an accuracy. Of course, some may be guarded. "Yes, I know," their face seems to say, "but when are you going to tell me what's wrong?" My experience is that the older students look at my exercise as a setup to criticism. Under the discipline of this ten-minute, five-day exercise you will find that students have much energy to give you.

Principles for Dealing with Struggling Children

What follows is a laboratory approach to helping children who struggle with the necessary room structure or exhibit other problems. There are specific principles that will help you to overcome potentially energy-draining situations.

We live with our classroom children day after day. I try not to let my emotions rise and fall with them. Some of the children have had a bad day before they ever walk in the classroom. I used to dislike playground duty until I realized that it was my early warning system for observing the children. I saw actions and behaviors well in advance of their arrival at the classroom door. Sometimes, I had a bad day with some children and then dreaded their arrival the next day.

I'd like to introduce some principles for dealing with children who present emotionally draining problems.

Begin Today as If Yesterday Did Not Exist

I know, this is like being asked not to think about a purple cow. Young children have often forgotten about the problems of the day before. But we remember yesterday and we have already adopted a defensive structure that reminds them of yesterday's problem. We have to practice forgetting.

Years ago, I learned that it was important to include children with learning or emotional problems in a demonstration before teacher observers. I deliberately asked not to have the problem children identified. Problem children can tell in an instant when I had no preconceived ideas about their abilities. I began my workshop very much like the invitation you tried when listening and responding to what children could do. These children would make me look like a superior teacher simply because I demonstrated no prior knowledge of their behaviors. The children quickly discerned that I knew nothing about their past and grew more expansive in their responses.

Attend to Problem Children Early

This principle moves me to attend to a child well before problems arise. This means I am listening or chatting with these children when they enter in the morning. I am reading the situation before any issues arise that require me to respond when the children are misbehaving or misdirected in their learning. Attending to misbehavior when it occurs is merely reinforcing that behavior.

I find that in any classroom there are usually three or four children who fall into this category. A study done long ago in New York City showed that psychically we only carry that many children in mind. The researcher in that study asked, "List your problem children." In the best and most difficult of classrooms four children was the statistical limit. It also meant that as soon as one of the four moved away, another occupied the place of the problem child.

Give More Time to Children Who Affect
the Total Life of the Classroom

For good or ill, there are usually three or four children who affect the social climate of the classroom. I spend more time with them to steer their influence in productive ways. I may ask them, "What's a better way to use our time on this? What new jobs do you think we may be able to introduce to the class?"

Take a few moments to examine objectively your class roster to identify these children. They may be identified in some of the following ways:

- Aggressive children who pull other children with them
- Class clowns or entertainers who introduce levity
- Children who are particularly good in sports
- Born leader children who are often voted class president; they are thoughtful of others and many want them to be their friend
- Children outwardly handsome in appearance
- Highly intelligent children who lead with their intelligence.

You may disagree with certain children's behaviors, but objectively you know they often influence the direction of your teaching or the climate of the room. This is not to say that all children aren't important and have equal value. I know, however, that my time will be well spent if I focus on those who are leaders.

Of course, some children affect a room's direction and have few followers. I think specifically of children who have severe emotional problems. That is, at any moment they can cause a sudden explosion in the room. You and the class are either in the middle of an explosion or fearing that one might occur at any moment. Children who have these types of problems are often isolated because of their unpredictability. My greatest challenge is to somehow find a child who may be a potential friend of the problem child. I can't choose a friend, but I can observe the problem child sustaining some effective work and exercising cooperative behavior, however short.

Expand Your Sphere of Contacts for Difficult Problems

This is an important principle to follow when working with the problem child. I may include another teacher with whom I have built a special relationship (see Chapter 6). I have a particular approach I use with my colleagues. I make my approach to my colleague as constructive and objective as I can, saving my emotional sharing for later. The process I use works something like the following:

> *Don:* Amanda, I need you to listen to me tell about Antonio because I'm having a real rough time figuring what to do. I'm going to describe the situation as best I can and would you tell me back as clearly as you can what I'm saying. Maybe after telling you and getting the thing out of my head I can see the situation more clearly. Right now it's all a muddle and what I'm doing just isn't working.
>
> Antonio enjoys picking on children smaller than himself. He doesn't do it in front of me or when I'm looking. He does this on the bus, playground, or in a cafeteria line. Children come to me in tears and Antonio's simple response is, "I didn't do nothin'."

I try to be as specific as I can describing the behavior without opinion, though I'm sure I've probably arranged my description to demonstrate my powerlessness.

If I don't go to my colleague, I'll try the special education person, or even the principal. Usually, it works best for me to consult with one person at a time. Increasing my contacts is a good principle for solving the problem and returning energy to myself.

What You Pay Attention to, You Reinforce

If I continue to call attention to Antonio's behavior when he picks on children smaller than himself, he will continue to do this. If I keep saying, "Stop picking on Andrew; leave Claudio alone," this is the best assurance he will continue his behavior because he wants attention.

When I was a doctoral student at the University of Buffalo, another student named Spencer did a careful study to prove this principle. He studied the mouthing behaviors of kindergarten children as children in those early years are often chewing on various items in the classroom. He got a baseline of the incidence of mouthing behaviors and then requested that the teacher try to prevent children from their chewing, "John, take your fingers out of your mouth. Samantha, those crayons were meant for coloring, not chewing. Jason, I've told you once, I've told you twice, that book binding isn't going to last if you keep running your teeth down the edges." Immediately, the incidence of mouthing increased beyond the baseline. Next, Spencer asked the teacher to ignore the mouthing behaviors. The mouthing behaviors skyrocketed in their frequency. Children would deliberately stand in front of the teacher while chewing away on something because they missed her attention.

In the final step of Spencer's study, he asked the teacher to attend positively to something else the children were doing. Interestingly, this kind of approach brought the mouthing behaviors below the initial baseline reading. Above all, the children need attention. The important question is, "What kind of attention are we giving them?"

Reflection

The level of energy that children have for learning is set by the conditions in the classroom. As professionals, we are the most important condition in the room. It is our literacy and the quality of inquiry in our own lives that provide the tone and the quality of learning in the children's lives. So much of learning is picked up while observing another person learn and do things. The children observe us each day from September through June in the ways in which we solve human problems between and among children. They witness our demonstrations and our lines of inquiry in our reading, writing, and solutions to mathematical problems.

Beneath our demonstrations is a carefully structured room with specified limits for uses of materials, activity in centers, as well as their uses of general space and time. Children have responsibilities and participate in the organization and running of the room. If children are to exercise choice and expend their energy in productive ways, then their classroom has to be a reliable and well-defined place in which to work.

Children are constantly defining themselves and where they fit into the social structure of the room. These self-assessments require a blurring of personal edges through actions that allow us to enjoy each other in choral speaking, singing, or informal drama. Further, when a class looks beyond itself to helping others in school and out, it becomes more aware of its own power. A class that is too preoccupied with itself has a tendency to produce energy-draining conflicts.

Children in any classroom come from a variety of families where there is a broad background of permissions; some are highly autocratic or permissive, allowing for choice without limits. Others are physically intimidating or carefully nurtured. It is only natural that all children will probe to find the meaning of the limits you have established. Some, of course, will test beyond the limits and cause great energy drain from you and the other children, but there are principles of learning and strategy that can help restore and maintain the class to become an energy-filled community.

5

Tap the Energy Source in Curriculum

When I first taught, forty-five years ago, our curriculum guides were about fifty pages long. There were even some subject areas that had no guide. We complained bitterly that our days were too short for the amount of curriculum we had to cover. If you teach today, you know your curriculum guides are four times longer, yet the day is the same length. You also know that health education is far more expansive since drug, alcohol, smoking, and personal safety have also been added. This is the short list of curriculum that has been added since I first taught in 1956. Further, your day is punctuated by many more interruptions since human problems have become much more complex and the need to keep people informed has never been greater.

The Personal Curriculum

Curriculum is the sum total of the content of human experience from the time we arise until we go to bed in the evening. The word *curriculum* is rooted in the Latin word *currere*, meaning "a running, course" (American Heritage Dictionary, 1973). We encounter formal and informal curriculum as we move or run through our days; some aspects of curriculum we choose and other aspects we do not. Your curriculum is well represented in the full rendering of your week in Chapter 2. Each aspect of curriculum requires us to make decisions to learn and take in information for our own use. For every choice, there is a decision to reject another opportunity. Consider curriculum in the life of Donald Graves, a sixty-nine-year-old writer:

> Yesterday my curriculum began at 6:00 A.M. with a decision to heat coffee and check the long-range weather forecast for the half-marathon

race I would run next Sunday. I try to sift through the information by checking out a storm in Washington State and the southwest and gauge the west–east weather track of both. I know it is too early to tell. I respond to two e-mails that came in from California and Hawaii. I want to know what they think of the last chapter I completed. I sift through what strikes them and what doesn't. I want the book to be good.

At 6:30 I plan my workday over breakfast. I tend to have the same breakfast each morning. Keep it simple and nutritious, raisin bran. Tune into another local TV weather forecast. I still can't get the data I want for Sunday.

At 7:00 I review the day with my wife Betty. It is time to plow the garden for next spring. First harvest the beets. This fall curriculum has set rhythms: harvest squash, beets, tomatoes etc., "weed" the hemlocks on the south lot that are too small, rake leaves, bring in outside furniture from deck for winter. Each season has its own curriculum, new learning, and planning.

Writing begins at 7:15 and goes until 11:00. I brainstorm ideas for the curriculum chapter. I rapidly list every possibility and then begin to slot problems and solutions into different categories. At first no decisions, just a letting in, and then a forming into the best way to teach concepts.

At 1:30 I reacquaint myself with the rototiller as I only plow in fall so I have to remember and reacquaint myself with the safety features, levels for operation, etc. This is a review of an older curriculum not used nearly often enough.

At 3:00 I go to work to learn more about my tiny Palm Pilot computer. I call technical services three times and work with three different people who can't help me import files and use my global positioning device. My usual frustration with my electronic curriculum is showing. I know I am closer from their explanations but they cannot take me through to success. Each has a different solution that doesn't work.

Of course, this is an abstract of my curriculum. There are phone calls, other letters I have written, book discussions with my wife Betty, decisions about clothing, finance, this year's garden, next year's garden. It is no accident that the Latin root to curriculum is "running." Curriculum has a stream of motion to it that requires decision making and actions, both large and small.

There are times when my curriculum slows down, such as when I attempt to understand my Palm Pilot. (The palm pilot is a four-ounce, 2MB computer that fits in the palm of the hand and contains addresses, memos, short texts, maps, and so forth.) I read the manual numerous times and cannot solve my file-import problem. I know there is a solution and I immediately consult and find no help. Consultation and the willingness to admit problems is an essential life skill in the modern curriculum.

I am also active in planning curriculum. The energy of the curriculum lies in the making, learning, and planning of what is ahead. I felt energy in the exchange with my wife in the garden, but some drain from my attempts to get help with technical services at Palm computer.

Consider curriculum in the life of Karen, a child in fifth grade. Her curriculum is no less complicated than my own.

Karen arises to the alarm at 6:30 to catch her bus at 7:00. She is a bit out of kilter because the T-shirt with the image of her favorite rock group on front and back is still wet in the washer. The clothing curriculum is always a bit complicated as she has a few set pieces she always wears and she either can't find them or they seem to be wet or dirty.

She hurries to find her homework but the one key homework paper isn't in the book where she thought she left it. She feeds Binky, their pet border collie, her one chore before school. Karen wants to change the food because she saw a commercial that offered a broader diet than the one her parents have chosen. Just before she reached for the dog food she dropped two Pop Tarts in the toaster to go with her orange juice. Karen bolts out the door at 6:58.

Karen sits next to her friend Jennifer on the bus. They compare homework answers and talk about *Harry Potter and the Prisoner of Azkaban.* They gossip about Timmy who is renting his *Sorcerer* book out for $2.00 a week and already has three customers willing to pay.

Karen negotiates the "comparison" game with three girls who appraise and compare the boys, teachers, and girls on the playground regarding their clothes and looks.

School begins with homework check, spelling quiz. Her teacher reviews the curriculum for the day with time markers posted on the chalkboard. Karen dislikes spelling and feels a drain. "It's hopeless," she says. "I blank on that stuff." Reading time has Karen reading a story and answering workbook questions that include writing answers to comprehension questions and doing short-answer vocabulary work. Karen enjoys reading but not reading class. She wishes they could have books like *Harry Potter* and they could talk about them. She switches to math. The math assignment is on the board for her to complete the minute reading is finished. Karen likes the precision of math but dislikes the arbitrariness of spelling.

Science comes at 11:00. This is her favorite subject and she can tell it is the teacher's as well. The teacher shows it by engaging the children in actual observation of animals and plants. Karen's team has three pots of different soils and fertilizer and are conducting an experiment with light, water, and soil as key variables. Two other teams are doing the same work. Now Karen can talk and hypothesize with her teammates.

When Karen gets off the bus that afternoon at 3:15 she is greeted by Binky. "Sit," she commands. "Lie down. Roll over. Stand up. Good boy." Karen and her mother have been attending obedience school for the dog. She is learning a new discipline. Mostly it is self-discipline, because as her teacher says, "If I can train you, the dog will quickly learn."

Karen has many decisions that she initiates and controls concerning clothing, food, and friends. She is learning further self-discipline as she learns to train her dog. Paper-and-pencil curriculum is one that she does not control as much. Karen's teacher understands science well enough to provide some hands-on experiences in order to begin to think as a scientist thinks in the control of variables in her plant experiment. Consider some of the following as elements that contribute energy to your classroom. Productive energy results when children can knowledgeably:

- Plan their next step
- Make sense of what they are doing
- Understand the materials and artifacts related to the curriculum
- Construct their own curriculum in learning to be an expert in a knowledge area of their own choice
- Interact with other children and the teacher

We get a strong hint of where the energy lies in curriculum when Karen worked with her science experiment. Her teacher allowed her team to become actively engaged in carrying out the plant experiment. She took a "let's see what happens" tone when she helped the children to design their work. The children were then structured for surprise. Sometimes, science teachers communicate what the end result should be thus taking away any possibility of anticipation in their work.

Not all children like the surprise notion in learning. Their learning or family history has been one of overwhelming surprise and quixotic development. Such histories thwart initiative and produce fearful learners. Thus, the teaching challenge is to provide as much demonstration as possible within the structured classroom to allow for good child initiative.

The Importance of Questioning

I want to help children to begin to feel the power of successive questioning. It is one of the easiest places to open up child initiative as well as to help them begin to feel and experience what it means to know something well. Energy in curriculum comes from discovering the power of knowing.

INVITATION: Introduce children to sequential questioning.

It is rare that children have an opportunity to ask more than one question at a time. After all, there are many of them and only one of you. But the power and energy of real questioning is the pursuit of meaning through the sequencing of questions. You can introduce this concept through a demonstration like the following:

> *Don:* I've brought here an object that I'd like you to try to learn as much about as you can. You can ask one question after another, but I will answer with only the information that the question is seeking.
> *(I have brought a toy I had as a boy. It is a lead, unifomed sailor who is marching with a gun over his shoulder.)*
> *Boy:* How come it's dirty?
> *Don:* It isn't really dirty. It's just that the paint is peeling.
> *Girl:* What's the black thing around his neck?

51

Don: That's a neckerchief. It's part of the uniform.

Boy: Is he like a sailor?

Don: Yes.

Girl: How did you get this?

Don: When I was a boy, I saved up my money and I bought it to play with.

Boy: Why did you want it?

Don: I bought it right at the start of World War II. All the kids were collecting toy soldiers, tanks, and planes. Everyone was excited about the coming of war.

Girl: Did you fight in the war?

Don: No, I was way too young. I was only eleven years old when the war started.

This is a short version of a much longer questioning session. When the session was over I asked, "When did the session become interesting for you?" Students remembered that the question, "How did you get this?" brought the most information. When they made a connection between the person and the object, questions accelerated as they tried to recreate the history of acquiring the lead soldier. We discuss the power of "how" and "why" questions.

This episode is an example of helping children to begin to feel the power of questions. The ability to question is an essential part of the assertive learner. I also ask children to bring in objects and experience the process from the other side. They learn to see the power in questions to get at the information they want. Simply put, when children have many opportunities to ask questions, there is more energy in the classroom.

INVITATION: When children have gained more power by asking questions, invite a visitor to bring in special objects or materials for a question session.

When I was a school principal many years ago, I invited various people from the community to sit in an area outside my office with their materials. There was a sign-up sheet where children from any classroom in teams of two or three could come down and try to learn as much as they could from the visitor. We had no difficulty getting parents or community members as they had to give no speeches, just be willing to answer children's questions. We had a woman with paintings, a guitarist, a fisherman, garage mechanic, a woman just back from the Cape Verdean islands. The directions were simple: Answer each question, but do not elaborate.

It wasn't long before various classrooms wanted to have visitors whose abilities and interests were more closely allied to their own curriculum. The visitor would occupy a corner of the classroom. In this instance, the children asked questions in teams hoping they might get information or a "scoop" that would help them in their writing. In addition to generating energy and initiative in the children, the ability to acquire information from others is an essential life skill in the twenty-first century. The knowledge explosion is so vast that the learner of the future has to be adept at generating an individual curriculum that will suit their interests and abilities. A good reference in this regard is Paula Rogovin's *Classroom Interviews* (1998), in which first graders develop an entire curriculum through the interview. Her first graders learn to read and write, take notes, and publish their work from interviews with parents and community members.

INVITATION: *Introduce children to independent study through specialty reporting.*

Independent study is one more opportunity for children to initiate energy through special-interest work. This approach is a natural outgrowth of children's growing competence in acquiring information through the interview. When children come in contact with adults who are interested in their subjects, it is only natural that many children will want to pursue interests of their own.

I remember Brian Ashley's pursuit of his special interest in old-time whaling. Brian was in fifth grade and boosted his reading and writing abilities far beyond his level when he first began to pursue his interest. Brian followed his interest for several months, adhering to these requirements:

- Keep a journal recording what you are currently doing, thinking about, making plans.
- Maintain a list of sources for your subject.

- Interview someone who knows more about the subject than you do.
- Construct something that will help sharing the topic with the class.
- Prepare to answer questions about the subject.

Brian was fortunate to live in Fairhaven, Massachusetts, which is situated across the river from New Bedford, at one time the center of the whaling industry in America. He had access to many books and could interview an expert from the Old Dartmouth Whaling Museum in New Bedford. Brian constructed a small whaling ship and made papier maché models of various whales so he could reenact on a tabletop the process of hunting whales.

Since Brian's was one of the outstanding examples of a specialty report, I had him present his study in a small assembly. Other children would be interested in what he had to say because they were also pursuing specialty reports. It is helpful if an entire class or even a school is involved in special interests simultaneously, because children and teachers feed each other with the energy of learning. How well I remember Brian's presentation when he reenacted the detailed chase midst the rapt silence of the children. "Are there any questions?" asked Brian expectantly at the end of his session.

"Brian, did a whale ever sink a ship?" asked a boy.

Brian paced a moment, adding drama to his response, "Yes, the cutter *Essex* out of Nantucket was sunk by a large sperm whale off the coast of Chile in 1819. This whale was thought to be the famous Mobius Dick later referred to in Herman Melville's *Moby Dick*. Later it was believed that this whale was finally caught off Japan by two other cutters who finally did him in. Next question." The awe of surprise that followed Brian's statement seemed to awaken new possibilities in the minds of students for what it meant to be a specialist. I was as stunned at Brian's erudition and passion for his subject as were the other children.

It takes a number of rounds of pursuing specialties before children begin to see the power of limitation of various subjects. The common problem is that children choose too broad a focus and therefore have great difficulty in getting inside their subjects. They learn how to limit through your demonstration and especially the demonstrations of their classmates.

It is important to show the children how you pursue your specialty right along with their own. Show how you choose a subject on the overhead projector, then ask questions to show how you begin to open it up for study. Later introduce the various skills that help to bring in information such as note taking, using references, interviewing, and writing first drafts. Children have to be shown through actual topics. We cannot send them off on expeditions in learning without gradually introducing the tools that will help them survive.

I cannot say enough about the energy of knowing. There is that moment when a student passes from being outside a subject to trying it on like a coat that fits perfectly. Brian caught his vision from his interview. He witnessed the knowledge and passion in that man from the Old Dartmouth Historical Society. I have seen it, too, in a student who wished to study Joan of Arc and passed from outside to inside the subject when she wrote in first person as if she were Joan of Arc. You may wish to read Camille Allen's book, *The Multigenre Research Paper: Voice, Passion, and Discovery Grades 3–6* (Heinemann 2001). Her book shows many entry points into learning through one special interest expressed in poetry, essay, short story, and captions as well as in multimedia forms.

Time and Choice

One of the realities that teachers face today is the abundance of curriculum in relation to the actual amount of time to teach. Whereas curriculum has attempted to follow the exponential growth in knowledge, the actual time to teach in the school day and year has eroded significantly. Worse, there is a growing number of people who are distant from the classroom who speak of quality control through standards and testing.

The standards movement attempts to raise the bar without consideration for what constitutes real learning. The assessment procedures, which are often paper-and-pencil approaches to cut down on the cost of testing, do not evaluate the application of knowledge through performance. In short, standardized assessments have no way of assessing a student's ability to sustain thought on one subject for much longer than ten minutes. Our country needs long thinkers who can solve problems in medicine, society, engineering, and cyberspace. Further, our students need to see this long thinking in their teachers and mentors in order to begin to gain a glimpse of what it means to know. Instead, teaching to the test robs teachers of time to teach to know.

INVITATION: *Begin to ask questions of faculty members and administrators who genuinely seek to have dialogue about matters affecting curriculum and the quality of children's thinking.*

Consider some of the following questions:

- Would you choose two concepts that you feel are important in the field of science, say in the fifth grade, and tell me how you would know if the student understood the concept? How would you teach the concept so the student arrived at the understanding you describe?
- How would you know if the student understood the concept on a performance basis? That is, how would you have the student show you with materials that the concept was understood? How would you have the student show you with paper and pencil?
- How much time do you think it would take to teach that concept? In your experience how long has it taken you to teach it?
- In your experience what have been the best ways to teach those two concepts we have just been discussing? Who are the children who have the greatest difficulty in acquiring the concept, the greatest ease?
- What materials did you use that allowed for the greatest ease in learning them?
- What do you wish you knew more about in order to teach those concepts? How would you help another teacher to improve the teaching of these concepts?
- How do you think the application of these concepts will change in the next ten years?

These same questions could be asked of any aspect of curriculum. I ask them with the full expectation that knowledgeable people have already thought about such matters. I do not have to accept decisions from people who cannot answer at the conceptual/learning theory level. I do not have to accept the response that "they say we have to do this." I am the teacher of the children; I know who the children are, have a rough idea of what they need, and I need a translation of a standard or concept from a learning/developmental point of view. Yes, this is rocking the boat perhaps but I ask on behalf of the children because they are my daily responsibility and the source of my energy.

INVITATION: Choose an area of curriculum to see which concepts you and your colleagues or administration feel are essential. Consider asking which aspects of curriculum they feel are less essential.

There is an enormous amount of curriculum to teach and our time is limited. We have to know how to limit curriculum through integration as well as how we will successfully engage the children's initiative within the discipline. We can cover curriculum, not teach it, and waste the children's time. We can also choose essential concepts, teach well, and use time wisely.

INVITATION: Examine your use of time in relation to curriculum.

The best use of time is uninterrupted time. I continually work to help children be self-directed, self-sustaining thinkers. Every time I interrupt a child with a directive, a demonstration, or a message I interfere with the progress of their thinking. "You don't know my children," you say. "You have no idea how short their attention spans are. They are used to the TV hour where for every eight minutes of programming there are six minutes of commercials. They are used to eating at McDonald's and Burger King and fifteen-minute lunches in the cafeteria. They are like mosquitoes flitting here, flitting there. If they aren't interrupted, they are interrupting." Children's attention spans *are* shorter than they used to be. In addition, they are used to multiphase activity where they simultaneously watch TV, eat, glance at a book, and have a conversation with CD music blaring in the background. But we need to help children lengthen their attention span when appropriate. Children need sustained, uninterrupted time to use

57

resources, read, compose a text, observe and record in science. As you assess the use of time consider these areas:

- The number of transitions that you initiate in two consecutive mornings
- The number of times you have to give directions
- The number of times children interrupt the longer time frame
- The number of times someone interrupts your room from the outside via a knock on the door, an intercom message, a telephone call, a hand-delivered note
- Try to calculate from your plan book the average time for sustained learning by the children
- List the five children who handle sustained learning time best
- List the five children who struggle most to handle sustained learning time
- In which aspect of curriculum or time frame is there best use of time for sustained learning? The poorest use of time? Why?

There is a real danger in American schools to use our time to reflect the TV hour: assessment devices with multiple-choice answers, fill-in-the-blank responses, reading in short paragraphs. Long-term thinking suffers under these conditions. Worse, the student is set up to wait for the teacher to tell him what to do next. Long sweeps of time in a structured room allow for more independent, self-directed thinking, the kind of thinking needed today for the learner of tomorrow.

Reflection

We feel the weight of the amount of curriculum we have to teach. Curriculum has grown in all subject areas. Seldom do we hear, "This year, we will delete subject X from the curriculum as we take on this new material." As curriculum has expanded within subject areas, schools have also brought in curriculum that used to be part of family life such as dealing with drug use, smoking, domestic violence, and general safety. Although the curriculum has expanded, the school day has not. In fact, the school day has become more constricted through classroom interruptions, conferences, meetings, and the like.

Greater pressure is added through the standards movement and the addition of many layers of assessment. More and more administrators are pressuring teachers to prepare students for the test by taking tests. Losing three weeks out of the school year for standardized tests of all sorts is quite normal. This does not count the time lost where students specifically prepare for the test through worksheets and simulated assessments. Testing is not teaching. Teaching is showing and demonstrating to children how to acquire a skill and how to go through the process of thinking about a problem.

We have to ask tough, persistent questions of our colleagues and administrators if current approaches to curriculum are not to drain us completely. Currently, we are creating learners who learn to focus for ten to fifteen minutes at a time to prepare for assessments that expect no more than rapid answers. We cannot get off the subject of what it means to know, what essentials must be learned, and the importance of child-generated curriculum. When we adjust our use of time for longer learning periods in the well-structured classroom we are providing the essentials for significant learning today and learners who know how to solve the larger problems of our society tomorrow.

6

Build Energy with Colleagues

You wish you had closer ties with your colleagues. Instinctively, you know they can be a source of energy. In fact, you'd settle for just one with whom you could speak the truth about how you feel, share books, or swap ideas. But the increased pressure in schools, especially in the last five years, seem to make quality time with other teachers a fading possibility.

Ironically, on a daily basis you deal with more people than ever before. You speak with a guidance counselor, an upset colleague, the principal, a reading specialist, parents, and so forth. But rarely do you have the opportunity to speak with the colleague who helps recharge your own batteries. Husbands and wives arrive home emotionally exhausted from a range of unresolved issues. How well I remember driving to my home-haven from the university imagining an emotion-free escape. Betty, on the other hand, had a list of emotionally laden issues to review. Further, my teenaged daughters were usually ready to debate their need for the car, or an extension of curfew for the "once-in-a-lifetime" party on Saturday night. In those moments I'd recall my father, a superintendent of schools, who made the wry observation one frustrating evening as he dealt with my brother and me, "A school man has no damn business having kids."

Strangely, the less time we have, the more we ignore emotions and stick to facts rooted in policy, or "this is the way we've handled this in the past." Policy and history are important and do help us in making decisions. Still, we need to identify and share the feelings attendant to a decision. When people walk away from a meeting carrying unresolved feelings, they begin to know firsthand what it means to be personally and professionally isolated.

Teachers in this study continually said, "We are so far apart in our feelings. I attend team meetings and they not only disagree with how I teach, I don't think they remotely know why I feel as I do about my students. They feel I am too close to my students." Again and again teachers expressed how draining professional isolation felt for them. On the other hand, clear emotional exchange brought renewed energy.

These are difficult times for middle management in the public schools. I refer to principals, assistant principals, and curriculum supervisors. Boards of education and superintendents of schools are exercising more top-down judgments that transcend the boundaries of policy to affect instructional decisions. In short, more judgments are made distant from the child based on financial consideration, state laws, and the possibility of legal action without monitoring the emotional effect on the classroom teacher. This is analogous to the selectmen or mayor and city council deciding how I should raise my children at home or how I might spend my funds for their upbringing and education.

Take Charge

A strong colleague is too important in your professional life to leave to chance. When pressures rise that separate teachers from regular communication, you need to work even more actively to establish a relationship with one colleague that will help you to be the teacher you envision. You don't need a whole team, just one colleague. If you have no such colleague at the moment, become active in both locating that person as well as developing a long-term relationship that will mutually benefit each. Gradually, that one colleague will become a source of personal and professional energy, as you, in turn, provide the same energy for that person.

You may already have a relationship with a strong colleague, work in a high-minded team, or be fortunate enough to have an entire building that gives you energy. On the other hand, you may want to consider building stronger ties with someone to develop a professional vision for you and your students.

Whether you are reaching for a new colleague for the first time, or lifting your sights for your already-existing relationship, there is a certain initial investment of emotional energy to begin to move out from your present position. In short, it takes energy to get more energy.

What Teachers Value in a Colleague

I share a list from my research that shows what professionals value in a colleague that they consider energy giving. Consider some of the qualities listed below in order to attract the kind of colleague you wish to have.

Desirable Traits in Colleagues

- Has a sense of humor—is able to laugh at himself or herself
- Talks about children with specifics and how he/she learns from them
- Talks about what doesn't work; asks for help
- Asks for advice
- Knows more about you than just as a teacher
- Listens
- Shares methods and materials
- Shares books and ideas—talks about interests beyond teaching
- Has a vision for where he or she is going
- Is frank and can openly disagree with comfort
- Explores other points of view while maintaining his or her own point of view
- Volunteers; steps forward
- Is more interested in others than centered in self
- Generally energy filled

Working with the List

Some of you may say, "I'd settle for a colleague who embraced even one or two of these traits." You would also be correct in saying, "Hey, there's risk in stepping forward." There is truth in each of these statements, but there are different ways of exploring the building of a relationship with a colleague. I want to be especially sensitive to professionals who are in their first or second year of teaching.

New teachers suffer significantly from professional isolation. In many districts, new teachers are expected to produce the same gains in their students as those who have taught for decades. The result is that large numbers of beginning teachers are leaving the profession and with current labor shortages easily finding work in other fields. In an *Education Week* article (March, 1999), Jeff Archer quotes Richard Ingersoll, a sociologist at the University of Georgia in Athens. Ingersoll has analyzed U. S. Department of Education data and concluded the following:

> . . . in a typical year, 6 percent of teachers leave the profession, and another 7.2 percent switch schools. Surveys of those who left in recent years show 27 percent saying it was to retire, while a whopping 49 percent cited either job dissatisfaction or the desire to pursue another career.

Archer observes, "What he writes (Ingersoll) comes as little surprise to experienced educators, especially in an era when new state standards are demanding more of teachers, when student populations are more diverse than ever, and when more teachers are entering the profession before taking education classes or engaging in practice teaching."

First-Year Teachers

I began to teach without the threat of assessments and with colleagues who did support me, especially the principal. Yet, I remember the bewildering array of personalities in my thirty-nine students, the range of different parents, and the volume of curriculum to be grasped. I had trouble eating and sleeping and was short-tempered when I came home from school in the afternoon.

First-year teachers will need to consider access points for making contact with other teachers, especially beginners. The most obvious are before and after school. During school there may be special breaks, lunch, or even in teachers' meetings, where you'll have a chance to sit next to someone you wish to get to know. I am not speaking about extensive time commitments. Initially, the greatest need for new teachers is to know they are not alone, and that someone recognizes their place in the building. Simply saying, "How's it going?" goes a long way.

The next step to building collegiality is simply listening. When you ask, "How's it going, Jen?" take a posture that suggests no hurry and make eye contact. This kind of query most likely will come after school when you are both not feeling pressure. If you can, make a visit to your colleague's classroom instead of waiting for him or her to arrive in yours. Teachers continually mention initiating contact as an energy giver.

At all levels of our rushed society, there is a kind of doorknob communication. I acquired the term "doorknob medicine" from one doctor commenting about her own profession. Not long after I heard the remark I went to another doctor for my annual physical. We went through the exam and the doctor deftly explained the status of my health. He rose, went to the door, rested his hand on the doorknob, and asked, "Now, do you have any questions?" I had my list well prepared but only managed to get through the first three of a list of ten. I now fax my questions ahead stating, "These are some areas I would like to sit and discuss with you." Clerks, bankers, lawyers, educators from all walks of life feel the pressure of human contacts. Humans take time. More importantly, humans take emotionally laden time.

Not long ago I was in an airport when my flight was canceled. A long line quickly formed to make reservations for a new flight. I was worried that I might have to take a much later flight, as were the others in line. I noticed that the attendant at the desk focused on each person with a familiar pattern, "And how are you today?" If there was some emotional steam to be released, he didn't duck it. Next he commented, "Now let's see how we can handle this." In spite of the long, anxious line in front of him he focused on each person, calmly went about the business of solving the problem, and just as relaxed, greeted the next person in line. I was struck by his ability to focus, but even more on his calming effect on me and the other passengers. In any human sphere or workplace, the unhurried greeting with total postured focus on the person gives life and energy to both.

INVITATION: *Deliberately practice the unhurried, relaxed focus of greeting colleagues with special emphasis on new faculty. Be prepared for focused listening after the greeting.*

Focused listening means setting yourself temporarily aside in order to center on the person you are with. The following is an example:

Don: How's it going, Terrie?
Terrie: Got an appointment with a parent who thinks I'm not doing justice to her son's abilities.
Don: So, it has you wondering about her and the boy?
Terrie: I'm just starting out and you can be sure I'm probably not doing justice to his abilities.

Don: An impossible kind of feeling.

Terrie: But I don't want to appear as if I don't know what I'm doing. I want this to be constructive, but there's always the lurking fear, you know?

Don: I do know, and that's the challenge with each youngster. There are so many kids where I feel this gap between their performance and my teaching ability. They can do more, more, but how to pull that off; I'll spend a lifetime on that. Here's a few guidelines that have helped me with parent conferences. Tell me if any of this fits.

Notice that in this quick exchange, I put my feelings to one side and try to pick up on Terrie's. I could have chimed in on the first line, "Oh, you are having trouble with parents; let me tell you how I handle it." My first move is to honor her feelings: *"So, you are wondering. An impossible kind of feeling."* Relationships are first built on tone and feeling. Terrie's underlying feeling is, "Is this just me, first-year teaching, or what?" Make no mistake, she wants solutions and approaches. She's worried about what to do. We have the possibility of becoming colleagues when we can first share feelings. Terrie is probably wondering, "Does Don think I'm a poor teacher who will never make it?" I try to share my own uneasiness about dealing with the gaps between a child's potential and the actual performance.

This process of honoring feelings may feel quite unnatural to you. You feel stiff and mouthing words that make you feel like another person. This should not be surprising. New disciplines begin that way until their form becomes a natural part of you. After trying this procedure for several weeks begin to notice the effect on both you and your colleague. Notice the shift in countenance of your colleague and the energy shift within yourself.

INVITATION: Examine the earlier list of traits in the good colleague and consider trying some as an entry point.

Listening and Resonating

The essential base to being a good colleague is listening and resonating to the emotional tones of other staff members. Listening to a colleague does not necessarily mean agreeing. Consider now some of the following as easy entry points to establishing better connections with colleagues:

- *Ask colleagues for advice.*
  "How do you arrange your room for learning?" (This may involve a room visit.)
  "What are some things your students do on their own now that you used to have to do?"
  "What materials work best for you in reading?" (Science, math etc.)
- *Notice what colleagues do, wear, say.* "I see . . ." is one of the best opening lines to establishing a relationship.

As you go about the process of establishing connections you are looking for a colleague with whom you can move into areas that require greater trust. There is always risk attached to every one of the invitations listed in this chapter.

INVITATION: *Move toward greater depth in establishing a stronger relationship with a colleague.*

Consider some of the following as a means to being of greater support to a colleague:

- Share a practice that *didn't* work. Ask for advice on how to handle it better.
- Share a book you are now reading. Consider the idea of reading a book together.
- Ask for advice regarding a child who is not learning the way you wish.
- Discuss a risk you are about to take in your teaching.
- Share a practice that *did* work. Hopefully, you can rejoice together.

I tend to gravitate toward colleagues who have a sense of humor, people who can laugh at themselves or their circumstances. There is just nothing like a good laugh to establish friendship. And sometimes, when we lighten up, we find solutions to problems that might never have occurred to us otherwise.

Developing Support
INVITATION: *Work toward a more challenging relationship with a colleague.*

Good colleagues have strong emotional, supportive ties. Unless there is comfortable disagreement and challenge that extends beyond their relationship, they have not yet achieved the full energy-giving qualities available to them. Consider some of the following:

- Embark on a joint project in a specific area of curriculum or new practice. Experiment. Establish a regular time for joint meetings.
- Discuss a vision for your grade level or department. Begin to engage others in discussing this vision.
- You and your colleague start a book discussion related to a new vision or issue. Above all, allow for a wide range of opinion. Support and encourage this diversity. The rush to agreement excludes rather than includes.

INVITATION: *If appropriate, consider extending your professional contacts beyond your own local building or town.*

My research shows that many teachers who may have limited contact with other teachers move out to the Internet to establish contacts. Although I don't believe the Internet should take the place of colleagues within your building, it can certainly serve as a source of enrichment and emotional release and affirmation. If you have access to e-mail, consider visiting the following site:

CATENET: California Association of Teachers of English network. This is an award-winning network that began in California but now includes teachers across the country.

I find that many teachers even have dialogue on the Net with teachers in their own building or town. It is not always easy to have a face-to-face meeting during the day. E-mail affords access at any time of day and at the convenience of both parties.

INVITATION: *Review your relationship with your own professional organization.*

There is nothing quite like a trip with a colleague to a professional meeting to act as a renewal of professional and personal energy. Two of the basic principles to increase energy are contained in greater involvement in a professional organization:

- *Start moving*—get up out of you chair and walk; go visit another teacher, walk outside, call someone on the telephone . . . but MOVE!
- *Increase your geography*—go somewhere, make a new contact, get another point of view. Using the Internet is another way of increasing geography or attending regional professional meetings.

Reflection

Emotional and intellectual isolation is terribly draining. We have to make the energy investment ourselves to improve the emotional climate around us. A strong collegial relationship is too important personally and professionally for us to wait for others to come to us. Rather, we have to initiate contact with others because of its energy-giving possibilities. The more we take risks and learn from each other, the greater the energy-giving satisfaction. Ultimately, we see beyond our own limited collegial relationship to the possibilities of an energy-given vision we can fulfill together.

7

Create Energy
Through Learning

I remember the February day in 1983 when I was working on deadline to write a final report on my study for the National Institute of Education. The government had given us $200,000 to learn about children's writing and now I had to say what we'd learned. The harder I pushed at the data, the more I was blocked. I half-smiled remembering a friend's pithy comment when I was blocked on another occasion. "When all else fails, try telling the truth."

"Yes, but if I only knew what the truth was," I wailed, "I'd tell it." We had good data but whenever I tried to push them to explain small, individual differences, the data broke down. I looked out our big picture window toward the home where Jim, a professor friend, lived. Jim was a pomologist and just that previous fall we'd been out looking at the various trees in our yards. I was amazed at Jim's knowledge. He could look at a tree and explain any anomalous growth pattern, an extra limb, no limbs on lower trunks, the effect of trees nearby, the effect of light. To Jim no tree was the same. Jim's knowledge of the conditions for tree growth and the idiosyncracies of each species allowed him to see differences. Recalling that story caused me to make a sudden leap in dealing with my own data. Indeed, the purpose of research is to show similarities in order to see differences. The depth of the data in our three-year study allowed us to make general statements about children and writing. At the same time, it allowed us to see more clearly the uniqueness in each child, just as no tree was the same to Jim.

I remember the energy surge of that moment, passing from the despair of the unanswered question to the joy of knowing and explaining. Of course, the key is the unanswered question. If we have no questions then there will be no answers. The greater the question, the greater the energy from the knowing. In those days I was more than disturbed by unanswered questions than I am now. Gradually they have become my friends. A few years ago I wrote a piece, "The Writer/Scientist," for *Dragonfly*, a magazine for teachers and children published by the National Science Foundation:

> There is little difference between the thinking of the writer and scientist. Both observe phenomena and formulate hypotheses to connect the meaning of events. They are fascinated by data that do not fit the norm. Exception is the root of wonder, the unexplained the source of further inquiry, and unease is a sign of further exploration into the unknown.

You have known these same experiences. There are areas in which you possess solid knowledge, whether it be cooking, fly fishing, gardening, wildflowers, collecting antiques, skiing, or baseball. I know nothing of antiques yet I enjoy watching the experts on the public television show, "Antiques Road Show." Their broad expertise allows them to see the uniqueness of each piece. When you are in your own familiar domain, you know the meaning of an energy surge when you have answered the question that heretofore has eluded you. Of course, just as quickly as you answer one question, a new one emerges.

I've often pondered why energy accompanies learning. Why did I feel that sudden burst of energy on recalling Jim's detailed observations about trees and their meaning for my own research problem? Certainly, there was a kind of emotional release as the information helped me complete my report. But I think it was deeper than that. I had long been bothered by the uses of statistical data to explain human similarities. Now I could see how our data helped us to understand the uniqueness of each learner. The knowledge was fresh, new, and shiny. I was struck by the wonder of the newness.

Lewis Thomas, the noted neurophysiologist, who used to write a regular column for the *New England Journal of Medicine*, enjoyed the study and meaning of words. Thomas wrote, "Wonder is a word to wonder about. It contains a mixture of messages: something marvelous and miraculous, surprising, raising unanswerable questions about itself, making the observer wonder, even raising skeptical questions like, 'I wonder about that.' Miraculous and marvelous are clues, both words come from an ancient Indo-European root meaning simply to smile or laugh." Think how many times you have laughed or smiled just at the point of learning something new. Both learning and laughter are great sources of energy.

The Roots of Your Learning

In this chapter you will explore the roots of your learning. You began to explore your history in Chapter 3 when you examined what you did well and what you wished to learn. Although we may be going over some of the same ground in the invitations in this chapter, our focus will be more on understanding the connection between energy and learning in your life. You will take what you find and use your discovery as a means to help learning be a richer source of energy in your life.

INVITATION: *Make a list of the learning you've enjoyed in your life. Try to include the teacher, if possible.*

You will try to get a sense of personal history about learning. In this case I mean learning that you thoroughly enjoyed, from as far back as you can remember. Learning in this case refers to a body of knowledge or a particular skill you exercised well. Enjoyment usually means you pursued it with a passion, felt the release of energy, or you often thought about the learning when you weren't doing it. Here is my learning list:

- How to skull a boat with one oar; Uncle Nelson
- U. S. Coast Guard—how to row a surfboat; boatswain's mate first class Glenn
- U. S. Coast Guard—how to fight a gasoline fire with a fog nozzle; BM1 Glenn
- Maintain pins showing war battles in three theatres during World War II
- Identifying airplanes during WWII; Mother
- Hybridizing gladiolas; Father
- Russian geography, literature, history, and politics
- Running—35 years
- Anatomy and medicine
- Baseball—lifelong obsession with Red Sox

- Oil painting—I've only done one painting but want to get back to it
- Business, marketing, and finance
- Weather and weather records—I've kept a daily weather record for years
- Trees, wildlife, and ecology; wife, Betty; Peter Benson, Nature Conservancy
- Cross country skiing, skating; Jane Hansen
- Bible—Old and New Testament; Prof. Barth, seminary, Rev. Gary Demarest
- Writing; Donald Murray
- Writing poetry; Mekeel McBride

Some of these interests were short-term skills, but the joy of learning them was significant. Usually with skills there is a teacher/mentor. Again the purpose of this is to begin to appreciate what you have learned and perhaps the relationship of your learning to a mentor. In some cases, you may have decided to learn something on our own, and took on a field by yourself. The latter would be more of an independent style of learning.

INVITATION: Begin to get a sense of yourself as a learner through learning stories.

I want to take a closer look at myself as a learner, both in the distant and immediate past. You may wish to use some learning stories based on particular skills mentioned in your learning list. I already have a general sense of this, but I want to reach for more specifics about how I go about learning and how energy enters into the process. Try to spread out your recollections of learning episodes. For example, I'll choose learning in different decades like the following:

- Age 12: Learn about the B-17 bomber during World War II
- Age 33: Learn to do Biblical exegesis in seminary
- Age 50: Learn to write a book
- Age 54: Learn to use a computer

As I write briefly about each, I'll be curious about a number of factors to consider in the process of learning: teachers or helpers, the process I used, a sense of play in the process, as well as adjustments. I'll then try to summarize what I notice about myself as a learner.

1. *Learning about flying in war time.* Age 12: I sent away for a cardboard replica of the control panel of a B17 Flying Fortress Bomber. Foot controls for the rudders, plus a steering column were part of the package. I acquired a large cardboard box, plus several other boxes in order to make a cabin and fuselage of the entire ship. I then set out to simulate the actual flying mission of a raid over Germany. Five other boys joined me as we studied our various roles as pilot, navigator, bombardier, waist and tail gunners, and so forth. We climbed into the box and spent three hours flying to the target and back. Like most boys during World War II, we played many war games but this mission was more serious than most. All of us figured that the day would come when we would ultimately have to go into combat of some sort. We spent a full week studying our maps, planning air speed and length of time to the target, a ball bearing factory in Wilhelmshaven; we studied silhouettes of fighter planes that would try to shoot us down, etc. This was a kind of deep play and I suspect that we would have been insulted had someone suggested we were just "fooling around." This was a kind of coordinated learning lasting several weeks. As each of us raised problems of weather, fighter intercept, and navigation we enjoyed the chance to show what we knew.

What strikes me is our ability at that age to sustain thinking and problem solving. We constructed the ship, assigned roles, and learned our parts. We only flew one mission. The process of doing this just once satisfied our serious play needs.

2. *Learning to do Biblical exegesis.* Our requirement was simple: Choose one verse from the New Testament and exhaust the scholarship on that one verse, then write our own interpretation. I didn't realize this was a graduate course when I signed up for it. I had never studied Greek but the other students in class had. I told the professor I didn't belong, but he encouraged me to stay saying, "What have you got to lose?" I quickly learned the Greek alphabet in order to at least use a Greek lexicon so I could do the word

study required for interpretation. The professor created a kind of easy-going, "you can do anything" atmosphere. I was also able to get help from other students and survived this course, one of the most important I've ever had. Without a background in Greek, the course was so far out of reach that I relaxed and went about learning. There is something about relaxation in learning that allows all kinds of experimentation and top-quality learning.

3. *Learning to write a book.* After three years of gathering data, I set out to write a book to show teachers how to teach writing (*Writing: Teachers and Children at Work*, 1983). I'd written two or three articles prior to this attempt. In my mind, writing a book was a huge undertaking and I made it so. Above all, I wanted to be intellectually respectable. I tried to write the research chapters first, taking at least four months to write two of them. The writing was terrible. Worse, I'd isolated myself in Scotland, away from my usual respondents. I quit writing the research sections and began to write the sections on teaching writing. The writing flowed and I managed to compose a chapter a week. I learned that starting to write at the easiest point in a book, even if it isn't the beginning, is the best place to start. There's a dictum among writers: "Just say it."

4. *Learning to use a computer.* I knew twenty minutes after first using a computer that I'd never return to my typewriter. The keyboarding was easy. But learning to save, print, enter files, and save files was a different story. I kept losing files because I forgot to save them. Sadly, computers do exactly what you tell them to do. "Fatal error" was a phrase I came to understand quite well back in 1984. People would say, "Use your help section in your program." Computer manuals and help sections are not help for me. I have not yet learned how to think like a computer. Fortunately, desperate calls to friends brought results. I'd roughly explain my predicament as sometimes I was just too ignorant to formulate the problem in order to get help. Once we could define the problem I'd say, "Take it from the beginning. Pretend I know absolutely nothing."

After reviewing these stories I realize that I am not a quick learner. Strangely, the one place where I demonstrated quick learning was with the exegesis in seminary. I took a "what-the-hell" relaxed attitude and learned. I tend to make projects much larger than they really need to be as in writing the book or in learning how to use a computer. Since both the writing of the first book and learning to use the computer were new steps, I exaggerated the difficulty in learning to do both. Writing books today is quite easy for me. I still struggle with computers.

What I note that is significant in my own learning is my ability to sustain thought on one subject for long periods at a time. The longer I work at something the more the energy builds. After an initial, more difficult investment, I pass from outside the skill or subject to the inside. For example, in the case of doing the exegesis I felt very much outside the process until I could move inside the passage where I began to understand the Greek. This was my first experience in going back to the original language and seeing a whole new interpretation in light of the history and other uses of the words. I began with that one text to feel like a scholar and finding the way to make my own interpretations of New Testament texts.

I am not a quick thinker; rather, I am a long thinker. I see that in my play as a kid as well as in my focus on the writing of my first book. I can lock on to one subject and not let go. One of the reasons I did so poorly in high school and in college is that both demanded quick thinking. Not until graduate school, with its demand for long thinking, could I be successful.

Energy was generated in each of these four examples. In each example I passed from being outside a subject or process to eventually living on the inside. In only one of the examples, the building of the Flying Fortress, was I immersed from the outset. In learning to do exegesis, write the book, and use the computer there was a long lead time before I could actually derive energy from the learning and feel at the center of what I was doing. Mihaly Csikszentmihalyi speaks of the quality of this energy in his book, *Flow—The Psychology of Optimal Experience* (1990). Mihaly points out that high concentration from an inside experience produces endorphins. Endorphins produce a feeling of well-being and a sense of unlimited energy. David McCullough, the eminent historian, describes the "outside–inside" phenomenon this way in his writing about the great Johnstown flood (1999):

Not only do I want the reader to get inside the experience of the events and feel what it was like—I want to get inside the events and feel what it was like. People often ask me if I'm "working on a book," and I say yes, because that's what they asked, but in fact they've got the wrong preposition. I'm in the book, in the subject, in the time and the place. Whenever I go away for a couple of days, I have to work to put myself back in it, to get back under the spell.

INVITATION: Consider your daily learning and reflect on it. Go back one day and consider your learning in the last twenty-four hours. Choose now five or six episodes from yesterday. Consider the emotions attached to solving problems. What did you notice about yourself as a learner and its relation to energy?

Each day you live a curriculum. You made note of your daily curriculum in Chapter 5. Between the time you get out of bed in the morning and retire at night you live a curriculum. For better or worse, you learn. You are affected by your circumstances and as much as you can, you go about transforming those events to your own ends. You encounter a problem, formulate an implicit or explicit hypothesis, and act upon it. You are affected by what you have done and that large or slight shift in what you know usually brings forth energy and constitutes learning. When things work we get a surge of energy. For some people who are more aware of themselves as learners the surge of energy comes when they have an unsolved problem. The intention of this invitation is to help you to observe yourself as a learner. Here are a few examples from my own log book:

> 6:30 A.M. Very hungry. Make blueberry pancakes. Measure milk—one cup. I won't measure flour as I can usually estimate by thickness what will give good rise. I think the weather affects relation of flour and milk so I'll gauge the feel. Good pancakes. It works.

> 9:00 A.M. Call technical services at my local Internet provider because my new e-mail package wasn't working. I confess that only desperation made me call. I feel so ignorant when talking with these guys. The night before, the tech guy took me through an installation, signed off, and I couldn't get back into it again because there was no icon to click on. My tech guy is getting to know me and in a calm voice takes me

through three steps to get an icon. I even anticipated the steps and now know the pathway for solving that. Within minutes I'm back online with a new program. Again, the pathways to sending and receiving, setting up a directory, are all new but I manage to figure them out. I'm beginning to feel that maybe I belong in the twenty-first century.

9:15 A.M. Go to work on this Chapter 7, first by brainstorming the day's writing.

1:00 P.M. Off to Merriman House, a local home for the elderly, to read from my book, *A War Comes Home.* I review the names and brief description of participants before entering the home. There are three men and I want to respond appropriately. My friend, Sally Swenson, has the men (in their eighties and nineties) arranged perfectly according to hearing and sight problems. I am amazed at the detail of her arrangements. I realize there's energy in admiration. I have decided that maybe the men could first talk about the 1930s and they really get going about the Depression, Hitler, and the impending war. I note that they talk to me but not each other as much. I feel a bit of healthy tension knowing I need to work on that. One man speaks of a draft in the room and changes his seat, another says he needs to lie down. Maybe they feel tension in this first get together. Fortunately, I don't delay and get right to reading the chapter on a Nazi neighbor in the thirties and they focus right in. I was afraid they'd lose attention at that point but the man who wanted to leave and lie down stays. I have much to learn in working with and enjoying these men but there was enough success to learn how to refine the best way for them to tell their stories. As they tell their stories, and later to each other, I know I will feel much energy from that.

Understanding Failure

INVITATION: *Begin to assemble a list of outcomes from your past that did not turn out to your satisfaction.*

Every learner has to understand the meaning of failure. Of course, failure is a necessary part of learning. Failure is a relative term. It suggests finality but in reality is only a temporary condition. Someone recently said that next to children's fears of losing a parent, they fear failing and being held back in school. Young children view this kind of failure as permanent. Many of us who teach, even if we may not have experienced that brand of failure—repeating a grade—have been schooled as bystanders to those events. How well I remember Gordon, a boy in my sixth-grade class. When he looked at his report card indicating he would not go on with us, tears filled his eyes. I was both incensed and horrified. Even though I was going to the next grade, I felt something. I had the same feelings the year before when my dog Rags was killed. My teacher did not attempt to explain to us why Gordon would no longer be a member of the class. When teachers work hard to build a community of learners, I don't think they realize how many unresolved feelings are left in the lives of other children when one leaves, dies, or is not allowed to move on with the other children.

Strong learners ought to be able to articulate what didn't work in their learning history as well as what was successful. Each of us has defined our own bottom line of failure. We harken back to our own school days, when the possibility for failure was ever at hand. "This is the test that I will surely flunk," I say to myself. "I just haven't studied the way I should have." To this day I have dreams about failure.

In high school and college my grades connoted (to me) success or failure, competence or incompetence. I was on academic probation the last semester of my senior year in college. I had a rough period in which my anxiety over failure produced more failure. I was about to enter life as a failure. In that last year of college I became a self-defined poor learner. I had been found out and my feeling was that I probably wasn't college material. I can certainly recall the emotional drain that went with that feeling.

Of course, I can recall times as a teacher when I failed to reach certain students or their parents. As a principal, I failed to help certain teachers or succeed in dealing with the behavior of children in trouble.

As you consider your list of "failures," try to think of them as events that took energy or gave it to you. I look back at my academic probation in college and realize that I built an entire career on those terrible days of despair. For most of the years following the failure I unconsciously worked and worked to learn and better myself. Strangely, I could not admit to myself what I was doing until I published my first book, *Writing: Teachers and Children at Work*. The burst of energy from suddenly emerging from my thirty-year purgatory was uparalleled.

Writing for Publication

INVITATION: *Consider writing for publication as a source for new energy.*

Teachers who publish letters to editors, write curriculum guides, compose articles, or even write books, experience untold energy. There is something unique about putting one's ideas on the line that produces a bottom line to the self that is hard to measure. Many, many New Hampshire teachers have published because they've learned that publishing is just a matter of telling the truth about students, learning, and themselves. Writing as an act redefines the meaning of failure. Indeed, children could learn more about learning through writing than any other element in curriculum simply because our first attempts never quite measure up to our intentions. Effective writing teachers never let the child lose touch with his or her intentions. At the same time, the teacher shows the kinds of skills necessary for the child to communicate the dream.

If you wish to consider publication you may want to examine pages 368 to 370 in *A Fresh Look at Writing* (Graves, 1994). I show different ways to start publishing as well as provide an example of getting started toward publication from your own classroom.

Reflection

We can never underestimate the energy contained in learning. The first energy for learning is contained in unanswered questions: Why did that happen? Why do these children not finish their work after such a good start? How can I learn more about how to teach children to comprehend their reading? How can I learn to cook Italian food? Before we learn, we are outside the full energy of knowing. We begin the process of acquiring learning over the long haul until we eventually clothe ourselves in the energy-giving powers of applying our skills.

8

Take Energy from Assessment

The misuse of standards and standardized testing is draining energy from the profession. Whether the teacher is an experienced professional or a beginner, the ways in which test scores are used in America is one of the most demoralizing, energy-draining forces in education today. Across the country, the misuses of assessment ranked near the top of everyone's list in my interviews. When districts insist that teachers take months to prepare their children to take normed tests with readings of short paragraphs and extensive work with multiple-choice questions, professionals know that standards for developing good readers are lowered.

There has always been a need to improve the quality of student learning. Every study that I have done in the last twenty-eight years reveals that in each case, we have underestimated what children can do. Our expectations have never been high enough. Fortunately, we were able to adjust after each study and expect more. The excitement of creating a joint vision with teachers based on our own data provided a never-ending source of energy. Sadly, the top-down management styles used to improve standards will bypass the vital energy force that only teachers can provide.

It doesn't take much intelligence to know that the hunger for numbers to measure proficiency is part of a political game constructed by people far from the classroom. First, we need to listen to teachers like this one:

> I think teachers everywhere are so exhausted and teaching is taking so much energy because we are forced to compromise our beliefs too often. There are so many things that contribute to that—politics of district, legislative issues, testing colleagues' philosophical differences. I think good teachers get tired doing things they know are not right for kids— things that go against everything we know about teaching and learning. It takes a great deal of energy to do this.

Another teacher spoke about how controlling the preoccupation with test scores can be to school administrations. The administrators, in turn, pass on the tension to teachers with specific requirements, like the ones this teacher mentions:

> I have to write out how I'll prepare my kids for state frameworks and to pass the state test. My plan will get read and then I'll get prescriptions back on how to spend two months getting them ready for what I don't believe in. It's playing the dual role of what I believe in and being a fake to some extent that is energy draining. What an energy builder it would be if I could feel I was on the same page with an administration that was into real learning.

Two more illustrations point out how difficult it is for teachers who teach in low socioeconomic areas. When normed tests have guaranteed failure rates, it is extremely difficult for tests to show improvements where children are already behind. They may improve but their scores can't show it unless they make enormous jumps. Two different teachers speak about this dilemma:

> In our town the local newspaper posts the achievement scores class by class. Next thing you know they'll do it kid by kid. My school happens to be in a tough area economically. And I think our kids do well under the circumstances. But the superintendent treats us like we're an embarrassment to the community. Of course, we all know he'll be gone in two or three years and his reputation is riding on the fact that he can say, "I boosted scores."

> In our state we train to meet certain standards in all subject areas. But the state education department keeps changing their standards on a yearly basis. It's a moving target. We have a wonderful principal in our school and the way things are going he could be fired if our test scores drop. Picture this, we have six or seven first languages in a lower socioeconomic area, and the state keeps changing standards. There's just no cooperation.

It's a rare state department of education, superintendent, or principal who doesn't promise better scores on reading assessments. "This year," their rhetoric implies, "we will raise our student's scores above the norm." Unfortunately, normed tests prevent everyone from going above the norm. The failure rate is guaranteed. As one teacher remarked, "It's like Las Vegas. The house always wins. They've set it up that way."

One thing is clear; the country demonstrates an insatiable appetite for scores on normed standardized tests, as well as standards themselves. Unfortunately, test scores, especially normed test scores, are the means by which the public takes the temperature of the educational establishment. It is not unusual for realtors to post on their Web sites either the SAT scores, or reading test scores, to show the quality of the community where a prospective buyer will consider a home purchase.

Evaluation as a Source of Energy

Evaluation ought to be one of the greatest energy givers for the teacher in the classroom. The best teachers evaluate from the time the first child enters the classroom until she leaves. Indeed, before children arrive they evaluate the location of materials, the plans they will use, the need for follow-up to lessons of the day before, as well as weaknesses uncovered in both their own teaching and the performance of the children who are their charges for the year. Teachers who design and structure their classroom for learning know what skills their students need. Above all, they prize the initiative exercised by their students and the full range of their expressions. When the non-reader picks up a book and tries to read for the first time on his own, or the smart reader who hasn't ever read a book is turned on by a new author, that teacher knows the victory and energy provided by informal assessment.

Part of any teacher's assessment is a running record system that shows what children are learning and need from day to day. Running records show far more evaluative detail and record, most importantly, the energy-giving successes of the day, than do periodic tests.

The Field of Assessment

Before we can begin to deal effectively with the draining aspects of assessment, particularly the emphasis on standardized testing, we need to examine the field itself. We need to know more specifically what standardization can and cannot do. Until we understand some of these basics and clearly know their weaknesses we cannot be assertive about how our children's learning is weakened. Finally, we need to know how to turn situations that may be draining into energy-giving events. Following this review of testing, I will show with specific practices how to deal assertively with the process of taking energy from assessment.

The Standards Dilemma

I taught a graduate school course, titled "Research in the Teaching of Writing," for twelve years. Students were to formulate a research question, review the literature, construct an evaluation design, gather data, and report their findings—all in one semester. I felt that doing research and reviewing the rest of the field of research about writing was the best way to understand research in the teaching of writing. All of these requirements were my version of setting a standard for understanding the field. One spring, at the end of the course the students sported T-shirts with the words, "I Survived 880" on the front. (The course number was 880.) I felt a tingle of pride that I had set high standards and the students respected what they had been through. The course carefully prescribed when each phase of research was due. The best students ignored my dates, either meeting them early or much later since they had their own pace for answering their research question. I remember the tension of allowing deviations in student approaches and due dates. At each point I worried, "Am I lowering my standards in allowing these differences?"

It took me about five years of teaching the course to realize that students' expectations were often higher than my own. When that was the case, I had to allow a wide range of formats and data gathering approaches, even to the point of reporting their findings. I kept redefining what I meant by standards. The students, who conferred regularly with each other outside of class, kept asking, "What's the reason behind this approach?" I'd respond, then they'd suggest that maybe another approach might be better. The basic course framework didn't change that much, but each person usually had permission to pursue excellence in his or her own way. As I look back on those years, I realize that excellence results when students are able to put their own twist on a task.

Presidents, legislators, state and local school boards, and administrators want to be known as people who have high educational standards. The statements collectively imply that we need to be tough in order to see real improvement. We need to expect more from teachers and students if we are to maintain our position of world leadership. All our students need equal opportunity to realize the American dream and a good education is the way to achieve it. The way to find out if our students are doing well is to test them. How else can we find out if we are improving? The numbers have to show that we are getting better and that we are on the road to excellence.

The cry for higher standards is accompanied by rhetoric suggesting that schools are in a sorry state. No question, schools and teaching can always improve. To say that schools are worse than they were in the past ignores data to the contrary. David Berliner's and Bruce Biddle's book, *The Manufactured Crisis*, as well as Michael Kibby's study from the State University of New York at Buffalo, *Student Literacy: Myths and Realities*, carefully point out, using the same normative data by the doomsayers, that rather than slipping, schools on the whole are improving nationwide.

As teachers, we need to understand the business of setting standards. We need to understand in order to recognize the strengths and weaknesses in each approach as well as to formulate our own questions and chart our own journey. Our source of energy in dealing with the assessment dilemma is rooted in a thorough understanding of its causes, the problems in standardization, and a greater understanding of ourselves.

Normed Tests

This is the most frequently used device to measure school or district progress. It is not intended to assess individual children as much as to provide a profile of a school district or a state. The test objective is to produce differences in a population in order to compare them with each other. The differences are produced through field testing of individual items. The test items that everyone answers correctly or incorrectly are tossed because they do not contribute to group spread. The test is usually timed, as speed of response is one more factor to develop a difference in test takers. Children who take these tests usually have to select an answer from four or five choices and fill in a bubble with a number 2 pencil. When the data are returned from these tests, percentile scores show how the district is better or worse than others taking the test.

Normed tests are only a gross measurement of student abilities. Consider a reading assessment that asks students to read short paragraphs and answer questions, or make judgments about word meanings. The standard they set is quite low simply because so many factors have been removed that good readers need to be able to do. Good readers are usually working with much longer texts and have built up contexual clues over a much longer period in order to understand specific questions posed. Of course, if the texts are longer, then those taking the test will answer more questions correctly. Remember, the test is out to produce differences. The normed test guarantees scores at the bottom and top of the group. What we don't know is how good is good and how poor is poor. It may be, for example, that none of the top scorers is reading books and understanding them, whereas a number of the lower scorers are. In fact, students who can read entire books and relate their contents may do more poorly on paragraphs that minimize clues to produce separation in the sample.

Multiple-choice questions most commonly used by test makers rely on convergent thinking. That is, there is already a predetermined answer requiring students to arrive at one answer. Our students do need to know this kind of thinking. But they also need to think elaboratively, design problems of their own, and give evidence of problem finding. They need to show conviction and respond with precise language about issues that concern them.

Good readers initiate questions and interpret the texts of others with texts of their own. When students produce texts of their own the scoring of tests gets very expensive. It is expensive because humans must replace the machine scoring. Many test designers will say that text production by students is unnecessary. They can already tell the superior student without the need for any writing. Normed assessments cannot discern those readers who:

- Initiate questions about a text
- Apply reading to other interests and fields
- Read books

- Do long-term thinking using various reading resources to acquire information
- Can discuss a text with two or three other students and arrive at a new understanding, or maintain understanding while discussing other points of view with which they disagree
- Can take an opinion piece and present an opinion with supporting arguments

Test designers would rightfully say that it would cost too much to gather these data about a district. There is a good reason why multiple-choice tests are used: They are cheap and competition is great to have a low bid to a state, city, or local school district. Normed assessments produce a horse race to nowhere and waste the time of both students and teachers in the process. The tragedy of normed assessments is that their standards are so low.

Criterion-Referenced Tests
These are the least-used tests. On a criterion-referenced test, there is a body of information to be learned and the test seeks to learn if the test taker knows the material. There is no guaranteed success or failure as in the normed testing. This approach is certainly more fair than normed assessment, because it is actually possible to prepare students for knowledge they ought to know. Students are less in competition against others. Their scores are based on how many answers they get right. Children will at least have a chance to show what they know.

There are, however, limits to criterion-referenced tests. Their formats often continue to use paper/pencil, multiple-choice approaches. We still don't know if a student is able to carry out longer-term work involving multiple sources and preliminary drafts in order to demonstrate thinking in a discipline over time. Further, it is difficult to agree on specific bodies of essential information.

The Standards Movement
At the outset of my career, I was very much involved in the standards movement. I worked with the development of portfolios for the teaching of writing. I liked the way the process began by involving teachers in trying various approaches to find the best ways to collect writing and evaluate portfolios. What began as a grass-roots venture has evolved

86

into more of a top-down venture in which standards are imposed on teachers and students. Energy for higher standards is generated when teachers in every school system are involved in the process. This means that the early work done to arrive at standards in writing can be used as a body of information to be consulted rather than used as a weight to crush innovation and originality at the local level.

I've heard the word *standards* bantered about in so many different forms that I decided to look into the origin of the word. *Standard* comes from the old French *estandard*, which refers to a battle flag for a rallying place. That is, there is a standard holding a flag around which everyone who has a common vision can rally. I very much like the origin of the word because it shows what's missing in the standards movement. The top-down imposition of standards will never work because the vision making has been lost. Sadly, when I worked on the standards committee I thought that once we had decided what needed to be done educators would see the ideas as good and run with them. I was wrong. Although we had some good ideas, the process of development must start all over again. Tip O'Neil, the senior representative from Massachusetts and former Speaker of the House, used to remind his colleagues, "All politics is local." To be successful, any educational movement must be local.

I find that the following factors also work against the improvement of children's learning through current translations of standards:

- The implication that teachers never had standards before the standards movement began. In short, there is little attempt to meld existing ideas about excellence with the new.
- The lack of clarity for why standards are needed in the first place. Somehow there is the feeling that setting standards for teachers and children will clarify for ourselves a new vision for the direction of America. Our current vision is articulated as, "We must maintain our position as the leader of the world." Why? What does that mean? How is that to be carried out? Strangely, in the midst of our uncertainty, we crave certainty through standards.
- There is a great rush to impose standards with the continual use of the word *crisis*. The *crisis* word usually means suspension

87

of human dignities, reduced dialogue, and the use of language that depersonalizes. Real change takes years and is always a combination of administration, teachers, and community working together at the local level.

- I find that most people who bring in standards have little to no understanding of what teachers face on a day-to-day basis in the classroom. Today teachers need more freedom to adapt to the daily needs of children than at any other time in the history of education in America.

There is nothing wrong in having standards, if standards are used as banks of information giving a sense of important components that make up a discipline. When local systems are able to use standards as guidelines or identifiers of important things to know for children's learning, they can be useful. The tragedy of standards is when people use them as weapons to exercise their authority. There is no historical precedent in American education where authoritarian approaches from the outside have raised the quality of education.

Naturally, teachers cannot work alone. But the creation of a vision of possibility that will lift our sights for children often comes with courses and cooperation with universities and state departments of education, along with strong roots in the local community.

For further background on questions about standards, I recommend five books and one source that you may not see as complementary, yet do allow you to make informed judgments.

Calkins, Lucy, Montgomery, Kate, and Santman, Donna. *A Teacher's Guide to Standardized Reading Tests,* Heinemann 1999. This is a well-written guide to understanding tests with a sound discussion of their strengths and weaknesses.

Harwayne, Shelley. *Going Public: Priorities and Practice at the Manhattan New School,* Heinemann 1999. There is hardly a reference to testing or assessment in the entire book yet the reader will find how the highest possible standards are reached with diverse cultural populations, with classrooms using a wide range of approaches—all with a common vision, love, and excellence for children. It is the best example of the power of democracy to educate at the local school, classroom level, that I have seen to date.

Kohn, Alfie. *The Case Against Standardized Testing: Raising the Scores, Ruining the Schools*. Heinemann 2000. This is a short, persuasive book showing how the overuse of standardized tests is seriously affecting the quality of education and especially the thinking of our students. Further, this book shows specifics about how to fight the testing movement.

Ohanian, Susan. *One Size Fits Few: The Folly of Educational Standards*. Heinemann 1999. This is a perceptive analysis of how damaging the standards movement can be for teachers and children. Ohanian pin-pricks bureaucratic arrogance and pillories the ignorance of group think.

The National Center for Fair and Open Testing (FairTest). An advocacy organization that recognizes that standardized testing creates and rein-forces racial, class, gender, and cultural barriers to equal opportunity and damages the quality of education. FairTest works to end the abuses, misuses, and flaws of standardized testing and to make certain that evaluation of students and workers is fair, open, accurate, rele-vant, accountable, and educationally sound. To accomplish its goals FairTest organizes testing reform campaigns, provides public education and technical assistance, and serves as a national clearinghouse.

    This is a nonprofit organization with whom all teachers ought to be acquainted. They have a Web site: www.fairtest.org; a telephone number: 617-864-4810; and an address: 342 Broadway, Cambridge, MA 02139-1802.

Routman, Regie. *Conversations: Strategies for Teaching, Learning, and Evaluating*. Heinemann 2000. (See especially pages 557–600 on evaluation.)

How To Bring Energy to Assessment

For years I ignored standardized testing. I either pretended it didn't exist or wished it away. I was confident that our local assessments were more demanding. I can no longer pretend that we don't have a national problem regarding standardization.

Here are some principles for dealing with assessment issues. The fol-lowing elements will be discussed in greater detail:

- *Relax and slow down.* Crisis mentalities want us to speed up, sus-pend judgment, and do as we are told.

- *Be informed.* Make it a point to study issues, take more time before making judgments. Be aware of what may require long-term thinking.
- *Separate the person from the issue.* It may be quite obvious that a person uses a policy for personal power and gain. The minute I get into the personal issues I have joined the other side and the energy will be quickly drained from me.
- *Listen.* There is never a need to answer a question quickly. Wait, rephrase a question, and perhaps ask a question in return to get at the reason the other person is asking the question. This is part of slowing the process down.
- *Broaden your professional contacts.* Don't be isolated. Seek help and don't be the only person who asks questions. Don't get off the subject of what is best for your children. Use the Internet. Attend professional meetings.
- *Ask many questions*, persistently and quietly. Questions are considered acts of aggression (to some degree they are), but the old passive stance must go or there will be no energy return.
- *Do not be surprised.* Slowing a process down often brings upset, a challenge to your credential of "just being a teacher," or an appeal to a higher order, "this is board policy, state policy, etc." Once again, you are asking on behalf of your students with specific questions relating to the nature of learning itself, a specific case where you know policy will not help the child. Your counter questions are quiet and persistent. You expect people to give professional responses that demonstrate a knowledge of children and learning.

Relax and Slow Down

One of my wise former secretaries who served several demanding professors mounted a sign on her desk that read, "A Crisis in Your Life Doesn't Necessarily Mean There's a Crisis in Mine." When we strode into her office sweating a crisis of our own making, that sign would stop us dead in our tracks before saying something like, "Could you have this done by noon?" Gradually, she created better work habits in the people she was serving.

In top-down management systems, crises are passed from one level to the next. The more lofty the position, the greater the power the person has to declare a crisis. Quite suddenly the legislature wants a report, the superintendent needs data for the school board, or the latest scores have been published and there is an urgent need to design a program to deal with supposed declining scores. The *crisis* word usually means a suspension of current plans, the compacting of time, extra working hours, and immediate action. It is the military equivalent of being called from combat readiness to actual combat. There is no time for dialogue or discussion. Indeed, there may be such urgent crises as in bomb scares or the influx of weapons into schools that threaten the safety of our children.

Apart from the safety of the children, however, there is no need to use the word *crisis*. One of the great drainers for professionals is to be in a constant state of combat readiness where our best energies are wasted to satisfy immediate political needs instead of serving our children.

INVITATION: Practice slow in-and-out breathing when confronted by tension or demand.

When you are confronted with a crisis or a demand, breathe in and out slowly several times before responding. You are deliberately entering a different time dimension moving from immediate demand to thoughtful consideration. You deliberately slow time down. The in-and-out breath can be very relaxing. In fact, it is good to practice this in minor situations before applying the strategy to more demanding problems.

After the act of relaxing, I ready myself for questions. I relax my posture and reflect the emotion that usually accompanies the other person's demand. "This is upsetting to you. You feel an urgency here. It sounds like this creates a lot of tension for you." The range of emotions may be diverse: anger, worry, panic, aggressiveness, or sadness.

Be Informed
INVITATION: Consider a study group to further your knowledge about standards and assessment.

When crises are raised about standards, you must be informed in order to know which questions to ask. Part of being relaxed and having energy is knowing the ground you choose to challenge. You have already begun to examine issues relating to normed assessment and standards, but you should continue to study the field and especially keep in touch with data supplied by FairTest.

Separate the Person from the Issue

I'll admit that when I see people using standards to seemingly further their own careers, and to use them as a means to control others, or to give and withhold money, I get angry. That's natural enough but when I start to construct an evil person in my opponent to boost my adrenaline for the fight ahead, I've joined the other side. That approach will quickly drain my energy, especially when I play the game of winners and losers. We have to take the long-term view that change comes about through long-term persistence. I have to be open to the fact that I may be changed by the person I disagree with most. When I changed the time dimension to slow down the process, to use listening, dialogue, and thoughtfulness, I entered into a long-term view that would give me energy instead of taking it away. I have also taken the learning stance. Again, if I thought one contact would produce great changes, I have joined the time dimension instituted by the person with whom I disagree.

INVITATION: Practice by yourself and with others taking the point of view of the person who may be on the opposite side of the issue.

Listen

Listening is an energy giver because it is consistent with the long-term view of not feeling compelled to respond or act immediately. The person I disagree with may take my listening stance as assent or a show of weakness. I have to take that risk.

My listening, however, is quite active. I continually restate what the person is saying. "Let me see if I have this right. What you are saying is that both teachers and children must be able to articulate the same standard using roughly the same language. And you have developed the standards that teachers must follow. Is this what you are saying?" When I enter into the discipline of active listening, I am doing several things at once. First, I am making sure we both can agree on what is being said. Second, I am showing that I respect the position of the person enough to articulate it clearly. Third, I am introducing a structure for dialogue. That is, there may come a point at which I may ask the other person to restate what I have said. I say that with the proviso that he or she may not agree at all with what I am saying. I freely admit that it takes a bit of artful listening and exchange to know whether the other person is able to restate my position. Some persons in power enjoy demolishing listeners. They perceive a great gap between their own power and position in the hierarchy and the position you now hold. This is always a risk.

Viktor Frankl (1989) tells the story of being a Jew in a Nazi concentration camp. The Nazis did everything in their power to dehumanize the Jews. But the day came when he realized that they could not assign his status or value. As a human being, he could assign his own value and ignore what was assigned to him by his captors. He had the freedom to define how all that the Nazis were doing was going to affect him. When he realized that basic fact, he took on new energy and power. As professionals we have the power to decide how others will affect us. There is much energy in that realization.

INVITATION: Discuss with other teachers how you assign value to yourselves and how others seek to change those values.

Broaden Your Professional Contacts
An important source of energy for dealing with standards and assessment issues are our colleagues. One of the effects of the standards movement is professional isolation. We are not brought together in order to develop a vision or to create something new. Rather, we are brought together to be informed and adopt what has been previously digested.

INVITATION: Create a small study group to look into the origins of standards and to look at tests more carefully.

Our first move in increasing professional contacts is to listen carefully to mutual concerns and then to be informed. You may wish to bring in a well-informed colleague or to access good sources on the Internet. FairTest already has a Web site (www.fairtest.org), and CATENET, the California Association of Teachers of English network, is also available for professional inquiry and chats. If you wish to enter into this relationship use: *jburke5@ix.netcom.com*. This is an award-winning program used by teachers across the county.

Ask Questions, Quietly and Persistently

I find that the management style in the standards movement is top-down. That is, a law has been passed, or a directive has gone out from state departments of education, or from the local board and superintendent that certain standards are now in place and that teachers need to give evidence that their children are meeting those standards. I find that good teachers have very high expectations for their students and their standards often exceed those proposed by external authorities. Their standards, however, are quite individual and require extraordinary artfulness both to engage the student and guide them on a learning path. A solid classroom carries with it an atmosphere of high expectation and support and gives evidence of great risk taking both by the teacher and students.

What quickly follows with standards approaches is the prescribed methodology for achieving the standard. Most supervisors are under the gun to show evidence that students are on their way to achieving the standard. How else can there be immediate evidence that all is well unless there is discrete evidence that a reliable approach is in use?

None of this is good for the learning of all children. I stress *all children* because it is our unspoken oath to provide the best of teaching for *all children*. As teachers, we must begin to ask questions of those who may not think carefully enough about what is best for *all children*. I find that teachers are drained because their unspoken anger has no place to go. The source of our energy will be in our actions and refusal to accept the status quo on behalf of the children we teach. We must ask questions. Plenty of them. And we must ask others to join us in this endeavor.

When I ask questions, I have to ask them with the expectation of dialogue. I want my tone to be inquiring with the respectful expectation that the other person has done much thinking about the matters about which I am inquiring. Above all, I have to separate the person from his or her actions and ideas. On the other hand, I expect respect in return and know that I am asking on behalf of the children I teach. My best hope is that I will be able to ask questions without an audience of spectators. That means I will make an appointment with a sufficient amount of time for dialogue. I recommend that you have someone accompany you to show you are not the only concerned person, as well as to have another listener.

Questions About Standards

1. Would you cite a historical precedent that shows that this approach to raising standards works for children? (*What you are looking for is a historical precedent that shows that top-down mandates have raised standards for children.*)
2. Let me tell you about X child. From your view of learning, would you tell me how this approach of raising the standard will help this child? (*You need to choose a child who may have a learning or language interference problem, a child with whom you are now seeing some progress but who may require a long time to go before meeting specific standards.*)
3. How soon does this approach to standards assume that she will meet it? (*It may be that an assessment will follow too soon. If the child fails then how will failure help this child? Be prepared to ask questions about the assessment device that will follow in another section.*)
4. *I ask this question if a specific methodology is prescribed:* From all the data that I have given to you about this child, from the standpoint of your understanding of teaching/learning theory, how will this help him or her to improve? (*It is most important to keep questions case and classroom specific. We are here at this meeting on behalf of all our children, not ourselves.*)

Our right to ask questions means that we have to be prepared for questions in return. For the case that you present above, it would help the session if you come prepared with running records, folders, or collections of papers that help you to be specific. You have already thought about your standards and the expectations you have about your children.

Questions About Normed Tests

Your objective in this conference is to be able to develop common understandings about what normed assessment can and cannot do.

Once again, you want to establish a dialogue about all the children. If possible, you want to have repeated dialogues, keep them relaxed, as you know that it takes a rather long time to develop a trust and common language between you.

INVITATION: *Ask two colleagues to join you to either gather information or discuss the current uses of normed assessment (if it is used) in your school district.*

Most test designers would agree that they often disagree vehemently with the ways states and local school districts use the data from their normed tests. To be fair to test makers, it is important to first learn how the data *are used* as a means to help educators. Once again, you have to keep in mind the bottom-line question: How can the data ultimately be used to help children learn?

After you have learned as much you can from your own impressions, your group will call for an interview with the superintendent, assistant superintendent, or the person who makes decisions about the meaning of the data. Doubtless, the person you call asking, "And why do you want to hold this meeting?" You will have to answer as honestly as you can. "We want to have a continuing dialogue about assessment that ALL the children we teach will benefit from a mutual exchange of information about assessment and the teaching of reading. We know what we teach from day to day and we also have careful records on each child, we'd like to talk about assessment in relation to our own data."

You may want to consider some of the following questions during this interview. As you consider them, remember to listen to the answers carefully, often restating the response to make sure you have heard accurately, and make your tone one of curiosity and genuine interest:

- How do you use the data from this test to make educational decisions within our district? (*For the sake of an example we will assume your query will be about a reading test. Ask about the following categories if they are not covered in the first response.*)
  About children? About teachers? About policy?

- How has the school board used the data in the past to make policy decisions?
- What process did this test publisher use to make up this test? If your publisher hasn't informed you, how are normed tests of this type generally put together?
- From your perspective, what do you think it is important to learn about what good readers are able to do?
- From your knowledge of the reading process and what good readers do, how close do you think this test comes to actually finding out who they may be? (*It may be that the district is not interested in doing this and that the test is used only as a general measure.*)
- How accurately do you think this test measures the ability of students from other cultures?

Again, it is only fair that if you ask questions, the person you interview should be free to ask questions in return. As much as you can, you need to have answered each of the questions for yourselves. Think through what you consider essential for good readers as well as how close the tests actually come to assessing those features.

Do Not Be Surprised

The questions you have asked may not necessarily be welcomed. To some degree, you have reversed the process of top-down management structures. You have tentatively redefined the meaning of power, for usually the person in the power position is entitled to ask the questions. On the other hand, a good administrator wants to know what others think and will take a welcoming posture.

I think you know your own local situation well enough to consider what risks you take in even asking questions. You have introduced a change in time because you have slowed the process of rapid, unquestioning adoption. Your energy will be in knowing you are doing well by the children and becoming more professional yourself. Indeed, you have left the drain of passivity to tap into the energy of becoming proactive. You are conscious of the fact that you have entered a long, slow process of beginning to reverse a trend that may actually lower standards and is dangerous for children.

Reflection

We can never forget that our first energy comes from our children. It is the day-to-day, detailed accounting of how well our students are doing that gives us energy. Others may design standards that are beneath what our students can do, or provide expectations so unrealistic that it affects our day-to-day teaching. We have to steer the right course that we know will help our children.

We are very much aware that many of the uses and misuses of standards and normed assessment tend to separate ourselves from other professionals. Separation comes when systems are imposed and dialogue reduced because of the press of time. We cannot let this happen. We need each other to help our children.

Finally, we have to remember that when confronted by a world and a profession that is in a hurry to get to an unknown destination, that we relax, listen carefully, become informed and ask tough, persistent questions. We relax because we know that we are on a long journey on behalf of our children.

9

Exchanging Energy with Parents

I remember my colleague's wry words as she gave me a sidelong glance, "I see you have Lucy Waldron next year in sixth grade. Lucy's okay but her mother is a real problem. She'll question everything you do. She's so afraid Lucy won't be top dog in the class. It's like she thinks Lucy is the only one you have to teach. She's one of those hovering hawks, beating her wings before she swoops in for the kill."

I thought about Mrs. Waldron during the first part of the summer but forgot about her until the second day of school when Lucy passed me a note. In near perfect handwriting, straight out of the best Palmer text, the note read, "I must have a conference as soon as possible." The note was short, cryptic, and demanding.

I thought, "Oh boy, here we go." I called Mrs. Waldron after school and made the appointment. The tone of our conversation implied that I probably wouldn't do justice to Lucy's abilities and there were certain indications from my first day that Mrs. Waldron had reason to worry about me as her daughter's teacher. We set up an appointment for the end of the week. This was just my second year teaching and although I was reasonably confident as a teacher, I had just enough experience to know there were many aspects of my teaching that needed definite improvement.

Mrs. Waldron did most of the talking. She said that Lucy had gone unappreciated through our school. She had high abilities that needed to be recognized. In addition, Lucy suffered from asthma, and carried a number of anxieties about being with a male teacher. Mrs. Waldron was raising Lucy alone and implied that they both had known some difficult times. After listening for nearly twenty minutes I made my first query, "Tell me about Lucy at home."

"She reads quite a bit and she does some rather remarkable needle-point. Why do you ask? What's that got to do with school?"

"It has everything to do with school. I'm sure you are right, Mrs. Waldron, we never do fully appreciate our children. Tell me about the needlepoint. How did she learn how to do that?"

"I learned it from my grandmother. It's always been in our family. I enjoy doing small, crafty things and I guess Lucy got it from me. She'd sit next to me when I'd work and I'd give her simple designs and Lucy took it from there."

"I think it is remarkable that you both do that together. Would it be possible for you both to bring in your needlepoint so you could show the class how it's done or maybe you could bring in some examples of your work?" We had a good year together after that. Luckily, I stumbled on to a question that I've since used throughout my years in education, "Tell me about your child at home." Naturally, I'm listening for something concrete about the child on which I can build. Ideally, I'm looking for something that includes the parent.

My one question, "Tell me about Lucy at home," was just a nervous, lucky shot as far as its positive effect on our year together. With forty years experience I have better insight today about the dynamics of that meeting with Mrs. Waldron and other parents. Each of us approached our meeting with a certain amount of anxiety. I worried that she would think me a less than able teacher. Indeed, in my second year of teaching I knew more about my shortcomings than I did in my first year. Knowing that Mrs. Waldron was outspoken about her dislikes, I wondered if she might broadcast to neighbors about the inept young man at the elementary school.

Mrs. Waldron had her own concerns. She expressed them more aggressively in that she felt the school didn't know what her daughter could do. In one sense she was right; we never know. But I also know from attending meetings with the teachers of my own five children over the years that I carry within me another question, "Does this teacher think I am a good parent?" Mrs. Waldron was raising Lucy alone, an event in 1957 that was much less common than is the case today. I was fortunate in uncovering a relationship between mother and daughter in the needlework. I was also able to document that relationship by a joint presentation in class.

My second question as a parent, and implied by Mrs. Waldron, is: "What do you think of my child?" We both want to know, before any focus on academics, whether or not you respect our child. If we can establish that base with specifics, then we will be able to work together focusing on the child.

Working with parents is much more complicated in the year 2000 than it was in 1957. I had no difficulty reaching Mrs. Waldron. She had a part-time job and I knew I could usually reach her afternoons when Lucy came home from school. Today, it is more common for both parents to work. It is not uncommon to have a grandparent, aunt, or hired caregiver to have daily responsibility for the child. Sometimes the most time-consuming challenge for teachers is reaching the person responsible for the child. In addition, language difference is also a more common factor today in discussions about the children we teach.

This chapter will focus on practices that will give energy to both teachers and parents. In turn, these same energies will benefit the child in his or her studies. We will rely on many of the listening practices we've already established in Chapter 8. I will not deal with all the types of contacts with parents. I will, however, focus on principles of communication that ultimately help the children we teach.

Types of Contacts with Parents

The types of parent contacts are nearly infinite in possibility. Some are requested by parents, others by teachers.

Requests from Parents
- "My child is struggling with (subject). What can I do to help?"
- "My child is having fights with ___."
- "Other children are picking on my child."
- "My child seems depressed and upset."
- "You (the teacher) are upsetting my child."
- "Could my child please be excused from . . ."
- "My husband and I are breaking up. We are worried about the effect on his schoolwork."
- "There's a court order not allowing my husband near Billy. Please make sure he gets on the bus and no one else picks him up."

- "My daughter is allergic to . . ."
- "You absolutely must change my son's seat."
- "I don't like the books my children are reading."
- "I don't want my child writing about personal things."
- "I want to know if my child's scores are competitive."

This is a short list of the issues that might arise in a teacher/parent conference. In the last forty years, more and more emotional issues related to home factors have entered into the conference. Stress in the home with parents having less contact with their children has spilled over into discussions between teacher and parent. Clearly, the emotional ante is raised and cannot be ignored.

Requests from Teachers
- "Deron is not completing his work."
- "Deron is unusually aggressive with other children."
- "Mark is destroying the possessions of other children."
- "Jennifer has made a major breakthrough in her work."
- "There is a need for follow through on . . ."
- "We need to discuss Jason's continued absence."
- "Emily doesn't eat any of her lunch."

Reaching Parents
I prefer that my first contact with parents be by voice over the telephone. This is especially true if our discussions will be of a serious, highly emotional nature. But even with routine contacts I prefer a speaking connection. I am calling merely to make the appointment and not discuss the matter on the telephone. I call because I want the tone of my voice to be relaxed and friendly. At the same time I state as clearly as I can the focus for our meeting: "First, I want to talk about Deron's difficulty in focusing on his work, but I also want to discuss this with the big picture in mind and share what he is doing well." The parent may ask if we can discuss the matter over the phone. I usually respond, "I could but our discussion will be quite general. We won't have the work in front of us, so I can show you specifically how he is both struggling and growing." I will always push for the ideal, a face-to-face exchange. I have to recognize that leaving work early can present a real problem for some parents.

There are some circumstances in which I could send the child's work home and discuss the work with the parent holding the collected work under discussion. Answering machines present the opportunity to establish a good voice tone, one that will later presage a good exchange. In some schools, a third party from the central office makes the calls for appointments with parents. In this instance, I write out the focus for the meeting as well as the promise of a broader exchange about what is working well for the child.

INVITATION: Set up a system of preferred contacts with parents at the beginning or second half of the school year.

Don't hesitate to mention your system of preferred contacts while asking parents to do the same. See Figure 9–1 for an example of a survey to go home. Naturally, you will want to adapt this letter to fit your own circumstances. Ironically, as technology has made people more available than ever before, people have become increasingly difficult to reach.

Conference Preparations

At the heart of successful meetings with parents is a successful record-keeping system. Although I may have a detailed book recording marks, I rely much more strongly on the child's collected work. This means that I maintain folders of the actual papers in different subject areas. They are there because I do not send them home. On the other hand, any time a parent wishes to see the papers, the collected work may be sent home but returned the next day. Both the child and I use those papers each day to note progress and formulate plans.

INVITATION: Spend time in preparation for a student conference.

If you have not started keeping student papers, try to build a collection over a two-week period, then call a parent with whom you wish to discuss their child's work. Before each conference I try to gather data that shows a broader picture about the child as well as the specific focus under discussion. The solution to any problem a child may have lies in what the child can already do. Sometimes I have to hunt with a little more energy than usual. I have to remember that the child, the

Dear Parent,

From time to time there may be issues concerning the learning or well-being of your child that require informal discussion or a face-to-face meeting at school. In addition, there are often very good things that happen that I'd like to pass on to you, or that you would like to let me know from home.

I prefer to be reached through the school office at _____ (Phone number). The office, in turn, will contact me, and I will return your call. I also have an e-mail address _____ for you to reach me.

Would you please fill out the following information indicating the best and easiest way for you to be reached? Please place an asterisk (*) next to the one that shows which one you prefer as first choice for contact. Please place a (#) if you wish this to be the number you wish me to use in an emergency.

Name: _____ Child's Name: _____

If you can't reach me please contact (husband, wife, guardian) at:

_____

Home Phone: _____

Address: _____

_____

Work Phone: _____ Extension _____

Work Address: _____

Cell Phone Number _____
e-mail address—home: _____
e-mail address—work _____

Send letter by child _____
Mail letter _____

I look forward to working with you this year and in staying in regular communication concerning your child's education.

Sincerely,

Figure 9–1. Example of letter to establish contact system with parents

parent, and I all need to know what *is* working, and what potential may lie beneath an apparent problem. Although I have a very specific focus, I have to carry a long-term view concerning the focus of our discussions.

I use a preparation sheet before a conference like the one in Figure 9–2. The first column contains notes I make before the conference and the second column, notes I make during the conference.

The conference record is designed to allow the application of specific principles that I try to apply to the parent meeting in order to have a successful conference as well as a good exchange of energy for each of us.

1. The conference needs to be both specific and general. There is the specific issue under discussion but it must also include a review of the student's full learning profile.
2. Using the student's folder or portfolio I must be aware of learning trends. I must review the portfolio before the parent views it.
3. Be aware of what the student knows. Before the meeting, I review the folder with the student to get the "story" behind the evidence. I ask the student, "What do you make of this? What's getting better? What needs improvement? What do you wish you could say about this collection? What will you learn next?" It is very important to bring the child's perceptions to the conference.
4. Take the parent through the same process as the child's. "What do you see in this collection from what you know of the child at home? What do you like? What do you wish was different?"
5. As much as possible, gain a profile of the child as learner at home.

You may wish to see a more detailed conference record of a writing conference in *A Fresh Look at Writing* (Heinemann, 1994: p. 348, Figure 21.1).

Sharing Information

At the end of the interview I will try to summarize the student's perceptions, the parent's observations, and my own. Above all, I want to include what I have learned from the parent that is useful to me. I may ask the parent what he or she has learned from the conference. I espe-

Conference Record

Student: _____   Date: _____

Conference with _____

Conference focus: _____

_____

PREPARATION NOTES	CONFERENCE NOTES
General ability	Does well at home, concerns
Examination of papers	Parent observation of papers
Specific skill needs	General skills in evidence at home, concerns
Understands—knowing edge	Learning next at home, concerns
Trends in learning	Trends in learning, concerns
Next steps	Responsibilities at home
	Reading/writing/home projects

Figure 9–2. Conference record

cially try to clarify any remaining feelings that we both have about the meeting in light of our next steps. I am hoping that the plan for working together that arises from the conference will begin to deal with some of the unresolved feelings.

You may be wondering how conferences can result in any kind of energy exchange for you, the parent, and the child. It is the specificity of the conference, the detail of the record, that allows for the energy exchange. I can usually bring both detail and humor to the conference because I have asked the child's explanation of all kinds of things from his or her perception of cafeteria food, to clothing he or she leaves behind, to why he or she is reading a particular book. It isn't long before the parent is commenting about his or her own perceptions of school information, or the same way the child creates self-expression at home. One of the basic rules of journalism is, "If you want information, you have to give it."

Of course, one of the ways in which I share information is with the child's papers. I'll take three to five papers in math, writing, or especially from the child's art portfolio and ask the parent, "As you know Timmy from home, what do you see here, Mrs. Brancato?" Naturally I have my own perceptions of the papers and I'll share those. There is always some kind of an energy exchange in the sharing of materials. Even when a parent is upset or disagrees with what is seen, that is still an expression of energy. Above all, I want a parent expression. Until then, I only have half the picture.

The Road Ahead
No conference should end without some sense of the road ahead for either the teacher, the child, or the parent. The road ahead comes from looking at the various collections from the past, noting the trends, and then choosing a focus for the future. The road ahead should include the specifics of how we'll deal with the problem in light of the other strengths the child posseses. It should also include an acknowledgment of the feelings that accompanied our discussion as well as how we will maintain contact. The following are examples of various kinds of conference concluding statements:

> So, what we've been seeing in Matthew's reading log and papers is that he was reading quite well in October and November making good book

choices. Certainly his letters to me about his reading carried good understanding. When I met with Matthew he just said he'd try to do better but I sensed there was more of a reason than he was sharing. I was bothered and you were surprised too about his drop-off in his reading. We both recognized that he seemed listless both in school and at home in early December. I had no idea that his grandmother was quite ill and you had no idea that it was affecting his work. Of course, you've been quite busy making trips to the hospital.

Your family is carrying quite a bit these days. I will try to make better contact with Matthew. I recognize that when he doesn't write, I don't write back to him. Actually, when there is a void I need to keep in better touch. Matthew is an excellent reader and we can at least talk about specific books he's interested in. You've said he likes survival books, and I've noticed it as well. Let's touch base next Tuesday at 2:00 on the phone. Are there some other things you feel we should have discussed and didn't?

This concluding statement surveys Matthew's history, the behavioral evidence that he'd just stopped working, and the teacher's unsuccessful interview with him. The mother has noticed the same listlessness at home and a plan emerges in which the teacher will write more to Matthew instead of waiting for him to send his letters about his reading to the teacher. (In this room, the children exchange letters with the teacher about their reading so that the reading is accompanied by written dialogue.) There is a plan in place but also a recognition of the emotions involved: a sickness by the grandmother, great changes at home, and now the additional burden of Matthew not working. Notice that the final word is given to the parent, "Are there some other things you feel we should have discussed and didn't?"

This next concluding statement is an attempt to summarize a rather "unsuccessful" parent conference:

I'm glad that we have had this meeting about Jessica's behavior in class. This is a first and important meeting. I've met with Jessica at least twice and then again today to discuss her taking of things that belong to others: a hat, a pen, a lunch. When I ask her how they happen to be in her possession she says, "They gave them to me, I forget, or I needed it." Mrs. Jepson, you say that the other children pick on her and this is her way of getting back at them. You have suggested that you can't sit around and do nothing and that she did that in the last school and her life was miserable there. Well, we do agree that Jessica does have the items and that she's more or less had permission from you to take them. Jessica shows in her answers that she knows I don't approve but she does have your backing to do it.

When I asked you about Jessica at home, you said she watches lots of television and that she does take good care of her cat, Frisky, even goes with you to the vet. That was a great help to me and I'd like to focus on that as something for her to share. You agreed that that might be a place to start. We both want Jessica to feel at home in the class and this is our plan, which we'll keep in touch with. You agreed that you'd talk this over with Jessica at home and I will have her share about her cat in school and we'll talk again next Thursday. Were there any other things you feel we should have discussed and didn't?

This teacher attempts to clarify the differences between herself, the mother, and Jessica. She tries to state without emotion the differences between them but both would like her to feel more at home in the class. It is hard to say where the class picking on Jessica ends and the cause for it, Jessica's stealing, begins. But, it may be that the teacher can give Jessica a different place in the class through her knowledge about her cat. In this instance the teacher is looking for a common platform on which to build and to allow them to have a good exchange of energy. She isn't going to change Mrs. Jepson's value system, but if Jessica's status in the class can change, there may be a new beginning for the child.

Reflection

Parents and teachers need each other. There are times when each feels drained by the emotional roller coaster responsibilities they must carry for the sake of their children. Each has potential energy to offer the other. The potential for great energy exchange lies in the specificity with which each focuses on the child. The teacher maintains collections of the child's work, noting carefully the strengths in the work and the places where further work is needed. Earlier the teacher meets with the child to view the work through the child's eyes, then shares that vision with the parent. The parent may see trends the teacher or child cannot see. At the least the parent will see elements of the home in the child's work, if the school is drawing on the child's life beyond the school.

Both parent and teacher bring histories to the conference. The parent may not have been a successful learner when he or she was in school, or may feel "superior" to the teacher and do little listening in the session. Teachers bring their own anxieties; "Will the parent think me a good teacher, or a good parent when I have their child during the day?" Both teacher and parent would like to be thought of as good parents, and each has very high aspirations for the future of the child they hold in common.

The last fifty years has seen a greater delegation and assumption of parenting duties assumed or accepted by the school. Increasingly, both parents have to work, are more difficult to reach, and more of the child's emotional burdens walk into the school on Monday morning. Under these circumstances more parent meetings are needed with greater clarity given to the roles that each must assume.

Teachers have to be the first to share the strengths and beauty of a child from the school setting. When a teacher shares Emily's terse statements, the poignant story about her dog, the help given to the new child, or winning the last leg in the relay race, that opens the door for a parent to share his or her own stories. When a child is struggling or has a major problem, all the more the teacher has to search for what the child can do in the broadest of contexts. For better or worse each child has an aspiration, a deep longing to become something greater than he or she is at the moment. When parents and teachers meet, there is great humor, poignancy, and energy in their exchange about those aspirations.

10

A State Gives Energy: The Maine Model

States can give energy to teachers, and Maine is a good model to follow. I received an e-mail from Brenda Power with a casual notation about a state meeting that suggested a different approach to helping teachers. Brenda, professor of education at the University of Maine, had just returned from a retreat in Bar Harbor, Maine. Twelve school systems were selected to attend on the basis of high reading scores on the Maine Educational Assessment and differing socioeconomic backgrounds. Schools were chosen for their differences in order to have data that would be helpful to the great varieties of schools in the state. She reported that the groups invited to the retreat were asked a simple question, "Tell us the story of how you got such good scores." That request got my attention because my impression of states across the country is that there is a push to conformity followed by a search for those systems who do *not* do well. In this instance, representatives of the state committee wanted to learn from the teachers.

The state uses a criterion reference system rather than a normative one. That is, they established the criteria for what constituted sound achievement in reading. If the child or system meets the criteria then the child has reached a certain level of excellence. The child is not competing against all the other children in the state with the percentage of highs and lows already set. In addition, more data are available for teachers and school systems to adjust teaching and provide inservice at points of need.

Brenda's impression was that their excellence was more related to energy than specific curricula. "Teachers in these schools are really a part of a community, and were respected as professionals. While they had latitude and flexibility, they were working from some sort of shared vision or mission." Brenda also reported that she was surprised that no specific methodology came to the fore as influential in contributing to excellence.

The simplicity of Maine's approach was very appealing: Ask the good schools from a variety of socioeconomic backgrounds why they think they scored so well. They were asking in a much broader way a question I've often asked students at all levels. When students were successful I asked them, "You got that just right. How did you do that?"

Dr. Connie Goldman, chair of the committee, confirmed these early impressions in her preliminary report:

> I had expected to see more emphasis on specific instructional methodologies as participant explanation for good student achievement. Instead they emphasized general ways of organizing their work as very important. I was not sure whether the recurrent theme of flexibility was responsible for these answers, but it was evident that there was a sense that we needed to see successful literacy programs as much broader than specific materials or programs.

I attended the board meeting of the group responsible for the retreat as well as the report to the State Department of Education. I was as much struck by their energy as they were about the energy of the participants in the retreat. The common battlegrounds that center on materials and methodologies were not present in this gathering or the retreat. The word *vision* kept popping up. Knowledgeable teams of people in school systems had worked together to develop a common vision that centered in children's reading performance. They had developed their own "home-grown" version of what would help their children become better readers.

Maine's approach seemed to be in great contrast to what I'd encountered in other states. Maine had a bottom-up process of gathering information to help inform the state. Rather than looking to see what had gone wrong, they looked to see what was right. Although they admitted they thought they might see a commonality of method, they went with what the data showed. In all of my data gathering, whether at the classroom level, other occupations, or with a school system, I've discovered that there is energy in innovation, a sense of knowing that what has been developed locally works.

The climate of discovery tends to bring people together. On the other hand, when teachers cannot fashion their own program and merely follow along unthinkingly, their energy is low. In short, discovery creates energy; conformity and orthodoxy drain energy in a professional situation.

Orthodoxies demand simplicity and certitude. Teaching is fraught with uncertainty. I was especially struck by an e-mail from Brenda Power in this regard:

> What we have lost is the right to be uncertain, to be tentative in our understandings about children and learning to be ready to glimpse at the alternative possibility around the corner. There are just so many certain people running around! I'm talking about folks of all beliefs and persuasions about literacy and learning, not just those on the far right.
>
> When you're faced with someone who is absolutely certain of the right thing and would adjust your behavior accordingly, you have no choice but to defend your beliefs (however fragile) as certainties, too. This is enormously exhausting work to deny how complex learning and human relationships are, to ignore the continual shifts in who we are and what we know. How freeing it was years ago to have the license to say, "I don't know. I'll watch the students and talk to some colleagues I trust about it, and maybe (and only maybe) I can find out."

Brenda is not suggesting that we have to wait until we "know" in order to teach. What she is suggesting is that we need more of a research approach recognizing just how many variables are involved in teaching when we work with children. We need to talk more openly and perhaps more tentatively. When ideologies are involved then there is an unnecessary defending of territories.

Where large amounts of money are involved, most states seem to fall in love with orthodoxies and freely expect certain approaches and methodologies, followed by the right materials. Sadly, the free market of ideas and local innovation, the lifeblood of teaching, are bypassed. Friedrich August von Hayek, the Nobel Laureate in economics, makes a point about the free market that I think applies to our own work in education. "The fundamental advantage of the free market allows millions of decision-makers to respond individually to freely determined prices, it allocates resources—labor, capital, and human ingenuity—in a manner that can't be mimicked by a central plan, however brilliant the central planner" (*The New Yorker*, p. 44).

Maine is a big/small state. It is the largest of the New England states but with the smallest population per square mile. There are only about 200,000 students in the entire state. Many U. S. cities have more students enrolled in their schools than the state of Maine. Teachers have to travel many miles to meet with each other at statewide conferences or attend workshops. And they do. Maine is a "small" state as teachers are well acquainted with good practice in other buildings, some as distant as two hundred miles. News of good teaching spreads.

Maine children lead the nation on the National Assessment of Educational progress. One of the reasons is that children do not get lost in Maine. Only 14 percent of the readers fall in the novice category. On the other hand, most of the children fall in the middle range with not as many as other states in the high category.

I was especially impressed by the close ties between the Title I administrator, the state department of education, local schools, and deans of schools of education. Courses are fashioned to fit local needs and are often taught on-site. Maine has few resources but what they use they use wisely and well. One of the conference leaders expressed it best: "Our focus has been on learning results as opposed to scores."

I find state after state focusing on just the scores and several large states rewarding school systems for scores with high-stakes assessment rather than learning. Teachers are driven to prepare their students to take tests by giving tests, just the opposite of focusing on learning. A focus on learning requires teachers to demonstrate and respond to the individual needs of children.

Maine's success has been carefully built over a twenty-year period. The state first focused on writing in the early 1980s. That was succeeded by an emphasis on literature circles in the late 1980s and early 1990s. More recently reading is the focus with a heavy investment in Reading Recovery. What struck me about Maine's evolution is that with each new emphasis, the state didn't forget the very important work that had come before. Writing and literature are still in evidence and therefore lead to a more complete and balanced language arts curriculum.

I find that there is often a kind of selective amnesia when new administrators appear at the state and local level. The hard work of other educators who have preceded them is forgotten. I call it the Bolshevic approach to education. "We must abolish the past in order to realize a more glorious future."

Maine does have a lack of ethnic diversity. Ninety-seven percent of its students are white, living mostly in small towns with still smaller schools than those in other communities in the United States. Maine struggles economically. After graduation, the top students often relocate to other states where there is greater challenge and an economic diversity to accommodate their specialties.

I will show characteristics from these Maine systems that marked effective energy-giving change. Consider them as avenues of experimentation and discovery for your own classrooms and systems.

No Overnight Success Stories

I decided to follow up on five of the school systems invited to the conference in order to get a more complete picture of the changes in their systems. I asked them to go back to their beginning points, where they sensed they were going in new directions. First, I was struck by their ability to articulate where they had been, where they were now, and where they intended to go. Second, I was struck by the length of their histories—eight to eleven years teaching.

To some degree change had to be slow in a number of these districts because there was no money to throw at their problems. The vision for change began with one of two teachers in combination with a school principal or assistant principal. There was no grand scheme at the outset. Rather, people began to consider modestly the kind of expertise they needed to affect children's reading. After a few years of success in their first ventures, a vision might begin to grow. When even partial success is seen in relation to efforts, vision and energy begin to walk hand in hand.

Administration

There is a high turnover rate among school superintendents throughout the country. Maine is no exception. In fact, it is difficult to keep effective administrators in the state because salaries are much higher to the south in Massachusetts, Connecticut, and New York. On the other hand there seems to be very effective combinations of teachers, supervisors, and principals who are able to sustain the building of sound programs. Most of the people I interviewed who were at the center of real change in reading had been in their systems for at least eight to ten years. In one city building the teachers interviewed the new candidate for principal, told of what they had done in the past seven years, and asked the candidate for comment. They were grounded in course work and theory and wanted to know if the principal could handle such a program. Quite clearly, the growth in these systems was the near opposite of a top-down management system. At no point in these twelve systems were teachers bypassed or excluded from the change process.

Teacher Expertise

Children became good readers in these systems because the teachers knew what they were doing. The state, Title I, and local systems invested limited resources in the preparation of teachers to teach reading. I was impressed by the coordination among university, state, and local teams.

Reading Recovery programs from the University of Maine at Orono played an important role in preparing teachers in at least half of the systems selected for the retreat. Reading Recovery provides a disciplined system of observing children while reading in order to understand a child's strategies. The teacher, in turn, leads a child into effective strategies so the child becomes aware of what helps him or her read. Although the Reading Recovery program is highly individualized with only a small number of children involved, the staff training has a multiplying effect as expertise is passed on to colleagues through discussion and workshops. Reading Recovery not only affirms that all children can read, but demonstrates that fact with difficult cases. In short, Reading Recovery contributes strongly to the vision of the possible with all children.

In each of these systems children did not get lost. One school had a "Swoop Team" in which any teacher could say, "I think this child is having a problem." Independent of Individual Educational Progress reports or eligibility for Chapter I help the child simply got immediate assistance.

I find it significant that I heard more talk about specific children and how they read than scores on reading tests. This a subtle but very important difference from what I find in many areas of the country, where I find a focus on reading scores first and individual children second. I think back to Mary Ellen Giacobbe's statement, "Focus on the writer and the writing will come." In this instance there is knowledgeable focus on how the child reads in relation to the subtleties of his or her approach to reading. This is the equivalent on "focus on the reader and the reading will come." I ask, "Does the reader exist for the test, or the test for the reader?"

Dialogue and Trust

Teacher talk was very much at the heart of developing the energy that sustained their visions. Good talk resulted when professionals had extended time together in a course or extended workshop. When talk was case specific, it allowed teachers to develop a language together. For example, much good talk occurred when teachers came together to discuss the rubrics for scoring writing samples from across the state.

One of the sad things about teacher isolation is the lack of a shared language. A shared language that is case specific allows for a genuine flow of energy. Not only do I begin to understand this child under discussion, but we begin to develop a shared perception for future discussions. Trust comes from developing a shared language about what works and doesn't work.

I find that professional language rarely develops in the one-hour or even two-hour workshop. The presenter usually tries to fill the time with verbiage and to tell all that he or she knows about the subject. In one sense we are not much different from young children, in whom the data show that the amount of language is directly related to the action of hands and arms. We need to do worthwhile things and talk plenty while we are doing them. There is nearly always energy development when there is motion and discovery in a workshop. High on the list of energy drainers was the lecture workshop or pep talk. Even when the speaker was entertaining, teachers were especially sensitive to the waste of time in attending.

When systems actually provide time for extended professional discussions, I find that the language changes. With a specific focus on children and learning such absolute adverbs as *always* and *never* are replaced by *sometimes* and *frequently*. Absolute adverbs dismiss exploration. When exploration is dismissed, then the energy of discovery is lost. Complexity emerges with the intersection of children and learning. With adequate time for exploration, we relax and delight in complexity.

Many Changes in Direction

As the systems steadily worked toward improving children's reading, there were many changes in direction. Reading the data meant shifting to newer approaches but not necessarily completely throwing out old procedures. Instead of revolution there was evolution. For example, one system embarked on a strong literature emphasis. The data showed, however, that more was needed than just literature. That didn't mean that literature needed to be thrown out. Rather, something extra was needed in reading. There is hardly any approach or system that works for *all children* or *all teachers*. Human variability is too great. In this instance, I refer to the variability of the teacher as well as the child.

Low Staff Turnover

Low staff turnover was one of the salient features in each of the systems where I conducted interviews. This was true whether I was interviewing teachers and administrators in rural communities or in city situations. It is often thought that with low staff turnover, the danger of an immovable staff is a distinct possibility. This may be true in general, but in the top systems I found that a stable staff meant good use of resources.

When there is low turnover in a staff it is possible to make changes slowly and build toward excellence over a longer period of time. The investment in staff is not lost, and over a five-year period a staff can grow in expertise in specific areas such as reading, writing, or mathematics. Further, when one or two new teachers are added to a stable staff they are more easily helped by the rest of the teachers.

118

I pushed for more answers to account for low staff turnover. It is difficult to point to any one cause, but I find that the following array of factors in these towns is interesting:

- Small school enrollments: 200–500 students
- Continued inservice work
- Community support and parent involvement
- An energizing vision for children's learning
- Faculty communities with little personal and professional isolation
- The slow development of a common professional language

If I were to choose one overriding factor from the list I would select "an energizing vision for children's learning." I want to stress that this is a knowledgeable vision, not based in just a vague hope for improvement but grounded in strong inservice and sound record keeping. Further, visions accelerate in clarity and possibility when the data show that current practices are working, yet still need improvement. If visions are to be realized, the staff needs to talk extensively about their children and what the data show.

It is easy to construct a draining scenario from my other interviews across the country. Top-down standard setting with scores taking precedence over learning separates faculty from each other. Worse, when scores are analyzed building by building and teacher by teacher without significant focus on help for real learning, communities are broken apart and not brought together. The very people who complain that the government and society have become faceless, or who get angry about punching in numbers when they call a corporation line, forget that focusing on numbers before children and their detailed learning have the same draining, numbing effect on the profession.

Parent/Community Involvement

Most of the systems I interviewed gave evidence of good parent involvement. I sensed that for many, this was an area they wished to develop far beyond where they were now. Although staffs are quite stable in Maine, the turnover of children and the mobility of their parents is very high.

One system conducted a literacy fair. Both parents and children were invited, with pizza served for the kids. They set up a series of stations where different parts of their literacy program was shared. Sixty to 70 percent of the parents came. This same system sent out letters to the parents asking them to evaluate the quality of the program. Parent response was very positive.

Another city school has a long tradition of parent involvement. Before school begins in the fall, the parents put on a fair and barbecue for new parents and the faculty. It is not unusual for school alumni to return and attend the event. In one sense this all-school gathering becomes the base for opening contact with parents throughout the year for various fairs, music programs, literacy sessions, and so forth.

When systems have real data about learning to share, especially from running records, it is much easier to interpret the details of learning progress in reading and writing. Simply asking parents to come to school for discussion about a test score is very difficult to do effectively, even if the number may be impressive.

As important as it is to develop a shared language among the staff, it is just as important to develop it with parents. I was struck by how hard teachers and administrators in these various systems worked to remove jargon from their language as well as to develop a common vocabulary. Parents cannot participate in a vision if they are confused by jargon-filled progress reports. Parent support can be a most valuable energy source for children's learning, but they cannot get behind what they do not understand. Schools would do well to keep track of their contacts with parents, monitor their language, and especially assess parents' understanding of their children's learning.

Reflection

Maine uses a bottom-up strategy for improving practice in their state. That is, they begin with extant practice, and use a variety of models to help other systems. Naturally, there were many findings that could be generalized across systems and that might be useful to others. It is interesting to note that no single methodology or material dominates their findings.

When local systems are free to construct their own visions, local energy and efficiency come in to play. Rather than systems forced to come on board to conform to orthodox approaches to complex learning problems, districts create their own informed response that is tailor-made to staff and children's needs.

It seems that the state sees its role as one that brings people together in order to learn from them and then to follow with the best use of resources. Although the state's resources are limited, school people have chosen to respond to local initiative by investing heavily in staff development. When staff are brought together under the guidance of knowledgeable professionals and focus on children's needs, unhurried long-term learning and change is the result.

11

A Portrait in Energy: Virginia Secor

"People wouldn't have called me a very good high school student. I remember discussing *Moby Dick*, a novel that just fascinated me with all its themes. I'd be seeing things no one else did but when it came time to take the test I'd only get B's and my classmates would get A's. We couldn't figure it out and not until much later in life did I realize I was a divergent thinker. For me, that's where the energy is in breaking new ground, going off on interesting tangents, following important leads, and just doing the next logical thing." These are the words of Virginia Secor, supervisor of instruction in five small, rural towns in north central Maine. Her towns are rich in Maine culture but struggling economically as much of the industry that once inhabited rural areas has gone south or to third-world countries. On average, from 51 to 60 percent of the children who attend these schools receive a free or reduced free lunch.

Background

What follows in this chapter is the story of one woman, Virginia Secor, and a team of teachers who demonstrate the power of knowledgeable, focused human energy in the service of children's learning. We will follow Virginia's journey as she continues to ask questions and pursues her own learning. Her learning is centered on extensive reading, her colleagues, and the astute observation of children. Indeed, the main source of her energy is learning and the pursuit of the unanswered question. Virginia began by teaching eighth graders in Hartland, one of the five towns where she is a district administrator of instruction. "I began with language experience and writing. I had a whole pile of questions: How could I capitalize on their enthusiasm, what is the role of self-expression, how can you open up to inquiry and still stay with the students?" Before this, Virginia had worked in special education and was an assistant librarian at Yale University.

> At Yale I learned what scholarship was. I learned how much I needed to read in order to be literate. You have to build collections of books if you are going to have real scholarship so when I went into that school in Hartland I knew what poverty was. They had no books and at that time no library.

Virginia went to work to build up book collections for her students and she went into intensive readings of her own, taking in the writing of Donald Murray and the New York Writer's project.

> I learned the importance of student voices in that period but I knew nothing about workshops or conferencing nor how to assess student essays beyond the literal level. In fact, I had kids who were immediately outdistancing me with their writing. They wrote and wrote but I did not know how to facilitate the growth of their own voices. Give them purpose. I just knew I needed to know so much more.

Virginia took a position in alternative education for difficult high-school students in Freeport, Maine. She volunteered to learn about holistic scoring.

> Someone came in to speak about traits in writing and it was a wonderful experience for me. It gave me one more piece of the puzzle. I learned how to schedule conferences. My husband was studying art and I took in his notion of portfolios and the simple questions artists ask: "What is your best work? What are the features that are in your best work that you would use to improve your other work?" So, way back in 1983 I was trying to figure the relationship between the portfolio and the conference as well as the creative process.

In 1984, Virginia moved back to the same school district she had left. She was rehired as a resource teacher in grades five through eight. She took a Calvin Taylor course in higher-order thinking for the gifted and decided to apply it to her resource room of slower learners.

> But I had a problem; my kids were writing about Hulk Hogan and a whole bunch of TV plots. I was using Don Holdaway's read and retell and I used that to move into Greek and Roman classics. I said no to those

terrible stories and the kids became fascinated with the classics. We wrote and rewrote booklets that we mimeographed together. We produced lovely murals. We changed the setting of the myths and put them into modern day. We created our own classics and the kids loved it. Because I taught in a resource room with the lower kids I could do anything to challenge them. One day the superintendent and assistant superintendent dropped in unannounced and couldn't believe what they saw.

They asked Virginia to leave the resource room and work with the entire system as a reading specialist. When she took the new job, Virginia was pregnant with her first child. She began to read Marie Clay, and as an anthropology minor and lover of Margaret Mead, she decided to study her own child and hone her own powers of observation. She was also pursuing a master's degree in reading and writing at the University of Maine at Orono and wanted to apply Brian Cambourne's conditions of learning as part of her new responsibility in the school system. "I was also reading Frank Smith and lots of adolescent literature," Virginia recalls.

> So now I'm out of the classroom and suddenly the system is my classroom. My new question is, "How do I look at the system as a classroom? How do I step back and look at the system as a place of social exchange just like the classroom?" Some of the teachers had techs or aides and I could see that not much was happening there. The aides were more like "gofers," go for this and that, and they were being used to generate more busywork for the kids. I pulled them out of the classroom in order to prepare them to really help with direct instruction and focus on individual student needs as an emphasis. This moved us out of the realm of text-driven curriculum to one of student-driven curriculum.

Focus on Writing

Virginia pondered where to begin and decided to focus on writing. "I chose writing because there was nothing for the system to have to let go of. It was brand new to everyone." She figured that if everyone was starting from scratch it would be the easiest way to build a community. She took some student papers and began to help her team become readers of papers looking for various traits that would make a paper good. Taking a stack of papers, she asked them to arrange these in piles, to scale them from good to poor. Using her former work with art she asked, "What makes these papers good? And what would it take to make these other papers better?" The team then applied this same process to students, asking them the same kinds of questions.

> What was giving us energy was we were getting better and better at finding answers to our questions and figuring out what good papers had in them and what the kids thought about them as well. The key is to make everything possible, not make the wall too high or too low. You might say I'm more of a stalker of good ideas. It takes a lot of patience and a complete trust that the student work will provide you with the script for change.

Virginia's credibility began to rise when the students' writing scores in grades four, eight, and eleven began to improve on the Maine State Assessment. The team kept learning and scores continued to rise. "We learned that you don't focus on the indicator and teach that; rather, you teach writing well informed by the best student work, and the indicators will take care of themselves."

Focus on Reading

The team moved next to primary reading. The fundamental problems in those early years were interfering with progress in the upper grades. "If the student has an internalized notion that he is a poor reader in grade four then you had to undo that," says Virginia.

The language arts committee went to work and studied the problem for two years and ended up embracing a workshop/whole-language approach. An essential part of this decision was to rethink learning and time.

> Our system has a way of losing its direction. We have structured schools in such a way that we've lost the notion of the child as the center of lifelong learning. We've compartmentalized development into annual increments that have factored learning to a given year. We have lost the broader understanding that learning evolves over time. Meaningful instruction occurs when learners need it regardless of the grade they are in. Under our current structure of grade levels we have in fact created a learning environment that has taken away a teacher's insight.

125

From the beginning, Virginia's team viewed reading and writing as parallel developments. During their observation of both processes, the team found they could make predictions back and forth between the reading and writing. "We did lots of talking, which is good, but there came a point where you just had to write it down. I wrote a guide with Karen Lylis about children's reading listing indicators they needed to attend to in young children's reading and writing."

There were some draining moments in this journey. One superintendent asked her to come up with a hit list of teacher techs that weren't as good as others due to a budget gap at the end of the year. "That was a zapper, a killer of good work. When you are asked to violate a trust it is a real setback and it takes a long time to make your way back."

There came a point where Virginia needed more full-time help if real, systemic change was to occur. "This was not necessarily a popular move with the principals. I asked for their best teachers to leave the classroom, be prepared, and then go back to other classes or schools within the district. I took Title I funds to do this. Ultimately, the principals could see the wisdom in this."

Energy from Colleagues

One of the main sources of Virginia's boundless energy is other professionals in her own system. She has a strategy that will ensure the source.

> I always work with the best teachers first. They don't need you but you need them. You need their enthusiasm, work ethic, and ideas to foster a climate that rewards growth and innovation. The second wave of change in any system happens with those who sit in the middle of the road. If they catch hold with the movers they are moving. If they see advantage in change, rewards for risks, and safety in growth they will grow.

Virginia observed that trying to change the unchangeable means you do battle. Battle then is seen as unsupportive, and in reality it is. "It is too costly to expend energy trying to move those who are not willing to move. Support the others and use your surplus energy to cel-

126

ebrate success. Eventually those who are resistant to growth will be isolated and feel unsupported so they will leave or come along."

Children as Energy Source

Although Virginia's first energy contact is the staff, both she and her colleagues' ultimate energy source is the children. Her model for both change and energy source follows a classic bottom-up design. Virginia's teams begin by focusing on one language arts standard as described by the National Standards. But the standard is determined by where the best students are at the moment. The staff spends much time articulating what to look for. They discuss the significance of the standard and look at papers or reading data.

> We begin to collect tangible evidence from the children that show where they are and what they are doing. A natural process that accompanies this is constant revision of practice. If a staff can look at student work objectively you come to realize that there's energy in the revision, "Oh, here's a better way." This is a very personal journey. It is all about getting the staff to question what they do, understand what to do, and do it.

Energy comes from seeing what works. In this situation Virginia has limited the focus, observed the children and their practices, and helped teachers to articulate their way to allow the data to determine next steps. Because the change is both bottom-up and lifelong, there is much focus on growth data but very little on outcome scores on standardized tests. This is not to say the children in this system do poorly. Rather, the SAD #48 district where Virginia Secor works was one of the systems invited by the state to attend the retreat on Mt. Desert Island to explain how they did so well on the Maine Educational Assessment. The focus is on continual, steady growth. "A focus on annual scores produces a different view of the child, more of a final state kind of thinking. We don't want that," she explains.

Create Movement

Last summer when meeting with Virginia's staff I couldn't help but observe, There's a lot of motion in this system with people coming and going, attending workshops, visiting, with staff bringing in resources and lots of talk. They launched into a further explication of the observation. "Teachers have to get out of their rooms and visit each other." Every time there is a workshop for the entire five-town system, it is held in a different building. An important part of the workshop is when the participants visit every classroom in that particular building. This means that teachers are continually getting their rooms ready for company as well as traveling from room to room checking resources, layouts, record systems, or aesthetics. Virginia further expressed her philosophy: "Don't leave it all to chance. Make sure to put teachers side-by-side for a reason. Everyone knows the physical arrangement of a room, or school, has an effect on things. Rethink spaces within a school. Visiting and movement help that."

Part of movement is making sure it has a face. The team makes it a point to mention the names of people who are doing things, and getting them to share materials. Virginia implied that if you have confidence in your own work then you can point to the work of others and use names. "Continue to name the system and define it with the names and examples from those that created it. To leave them nameless is degrading and will defeat the personal involvement so necessary in this work."

The Energy Supplied by Good Materials

Acquiring and supplying the right materials for teachers is an important energy source. There is nothing quite like coming up with just the right book or resource at a time when teachers need it. Out of one of the school exchanges teachers said that bookcases would be a great help for organizing and displaying books as well as making them more accessible to children. Forty bookcases were built and delivered to those rooms.

> If students are into process work they will need many books and will naturally select them on their own. But if your materials lack substance, and many of our classroom texts are specifically designed for the unsophisticated, then students will be working without the rich content needed to support their personal curiosities. Learners learn more when they are expected to reach into the content and extract from it what

they want to know more of. Working at the edge rather than the center of understanding is what learners do. Take that away and we tend to relax our thinking, get bored, or disengage from the work.

It is always difficult and a challenge in a system with little money like the Newport, Maine district to have enough books to go around. Drawing on her Yale library experience, Virginia has a central location for books that are constantly in motion to the right school or class.

The Currency of Student Learning

Since the focus is on the students and their long-term learning, I emphasize again that it is the qualities of the best student work that guides the perceptions of teachers. Rather than choose a standard external to the district, the team focuses on what they can see in their own children, the actual work of the children to catch a vision of the possible. In one sense Virginia goes back to her experience with the art portfolio approach: Describe the qualities of the best work and then consider what would need to be done to improve the other work. In Virginia's words, "What we have done is used examples of the best student work to redefine what is possible. We work collectively to define why these samples represent what we want. We save these examples and keep them in exemplar packets used by our staff in their workshop classes."

Virginia sees great danger in expressing standards in terms of bottom lines. Even when she talks about bottom lines, she talks about them only as descriptors. "Never," she emphasizes loudly, "talk about student growth as a number that stands alone without a descriptor. Descriptors for us are descriptions of student development that help students and teachers articulate growth levels that focuses on our standards. This process is quite positive and energy giving in that at the individual students' level, they are led by their best work."

Faculty Talk

It takes many cycles of reviewing student work and much talk before the details of best work can become part of the language of the system.

We have found this process to have enormous power in terms of creating collective understandings of what student-centered learning is all about. It is only after several years that you begin to address the larger issues of systemic reform based on student growth. The larger issues get at aligning curriculum, material use, teaching practices, levels of professional understanding in terms of district standards. Certainly if teachers don't understand kids won't either.

Virginia and I discussed how long a time the process takes. For many teachers it is a Copernican shift to read out of student work, instead of reading into it, in order to help students with their own writing. But, with the continual focus on student work, and many discussions, the process at least has a chance. The payoff, of course, is in seeing student work actually improving within the standards of the district itself.

Challenges Ahead

Many challenges remain for Virginia's team. The challenges are phrased as questions: "What can we do in our guided reading program to accommodate the interests of our lower achieving boys? How can we identify and teach key thought structures kids need in order to process information?"

The team approaches these questions with a reading/writing focus. In this sense the district is quite efficient in not wasting time by keeping the two processes separated. At the moment they are exploring a reading/writing approach to science with the lower-achieving boys. The second question about teaching key thought structures is one that applies to upper-grade children. In fact, they are using the top work of the intermediate years to demonstrate to upper-grade teachers (junior/senior high schools) the kind of thinking that will help carry their students forward.

In the first phase of working with key thought structures, the team asked children to write about their reading. Not surprisingly, all they got was a retelling of the story. Says Virginia:

We asked ourselves, "Is this what we want? Is this the thinking we want? Is this a standard we think is valuable enough for all kids to become proficient?" We wanted the kids to get into comparisons, connect what they were reading with their lives, and also to connect with the characters in their books. I tried to write a prompt that would require them to do this. For those who were able to actually do it, we circulated their work. The prompt I wrote was, "Over the past few months you have been required to read many stories, novels, or books. Use this paper to tell about one of the books you've read. Talk about the theme in your book and tell why the characters acted as they did and especially connect what is happening with your own life."

Of course, the challenge is always to allow the individuality of the student to drive his/her own concept of excellent work.

Energy Summary

After my visit to Virginia's school system, I read through my telephone interviews, written exchanges, and data and arrived at a list of her energy sources. I called her and asked her if my observations were accurate as well as to give her an opportunity to add to the list. Energizing factors were:

- A good question or problem
- Finding good sources
- Finding the right person to do the job
- Recognizing good people and letting everyone know
- Understanding data
- Process of constant revision
- Lots of talk and developing a common language of understanding
- Celebrating success
- Student collections and finding a tangible source for data
- Seeing teachers together and making good pairings
- Hearing kids talk about learning to others, hearing their stories

Reflection

Virginia and her team have created their own model for change in her system. One day in the midst of an interview I asked her, "Can you

131

recall a moment when this all began, when you decided you had your own way of doing things?"

She paused for a long moment and replied, "Yes, I was raised Catholic and one day we were asked to draw our concept of going up to heaven. I drew my picture and the nun came to me and said, 'You have the best drawing and I would like to give it a ribbon but there is something missing. Look at the other children's drawings. You will see they all have a ladder going up to heaven. You put a ladder in and we will give you the prize.'

"I said, 'No, mine is okay.' I didn't get the ribbon but I didn't really care. I had my own vision and I liked my drawing the way it was."

The Newport district generates its own energy because they know the true source of that energy, the children. The children's best work is the full staff focus and they let those children be the leading edge to showing both teachers and other children a vision for quality work. Their energy is also the byproduct of pursuing the next unanswered question as they all work as a team, creating motion within the system where teachers have high access to each other. The unanswered questions are also fed by a wide range of professional reading. The system is contained yet open to a world of ideas and solutions.

12

Energy in the Workplace

I wanted to understand the energy demands on our profession by interviewing and studying people in other occupations. I did this in order to understand how we are unique as well as how much we have in common with other professions and occupations. I begin with a story to help frame the discussion.

Betty and I were invited to dinner at a new neighbor's home while I was on sabbatical in Scotland. I asked him what brought him to Scotland.

"Well, I've been hired to oversee a failing chain of hotels here in Britain," he replied.

"How on earth do you do that?" I asked.

"It's quite simple. I call the managers of each of the hotels, make an appointment, appear, and ask one question for starters. Now you have to understand I have dual citizenship, United Kingdom and United States, so I understand tradition in business over here. There's too much tradition. My question to the manager is, 'What do you do to make a profit?' Invariably, the manager takes me out into the lobby to point out how he's done much redecorating, brought in a new computer system, and made modernizations. 'That's all very good,' I reply, 'But what do you do to make a profit?' I don't really care what he says as long as he connects his improvements to profit making. I usually end our discussion by saying , 'I'm coming back in a month and I'm going to ask you the same question, but I'm going to add two more: 'What do your area competitors do to make a profit? What business are you in?' "

My neighbor went on to say that his hoteliers had forgotten they were in the people business. "People come wanting a place away from home that's like home, but very different from home in a sort of exotic way if they are on holiday. When that person walks in the front door of the hotel he should immediately become a very important person.

If you don't focus your every move and expenditure on service to the well-being of the customer, you simply aren't going to show a profit."

Later he told me that many of the managers had taken new interest in their hotels and the people they served. He didn't use the word *energy*, but clearly when work focused on the customer there was a frame of reference to monitor progress. Further, managers began to get a reverse flow of energy from their customers that brought new life to themselves and their business.

I want to take my neighbor's three questions and apply them to education and potential sources of energy. I will also continue to explore the similarities and differences in the workplaces of teachers and other occupations.

The Business of Teaching

What Business Are You In?

The word *business* might get your hackles up a bit. No, education is not a commercial business. But some principles of business and management can still apply. My neighbor's question directs us to ask: "Who is the focus of your activity?" In our case, we would hope to answer, "the children." Another implied question is: "And what do you hope will happen with your children?" In short, to what central end do we direct our energies in teaching? Our energies are directed to showing children how to learn within a learning community. At every turn we ask, "Out of all that we have to do what energizes learning so that it will last?"

I don't believe we've properly understood what it means to focus on the children, our "customers." The teachers who have energy view the child as a multidimensional human being, a child with emotion, intelligence, and potential. They have a different way of seeing and hearing a child. Most importantly, the child usually knows he or she is seen differently.

Our business is children's learning. But learning about what? We want them to be better readers, writers, mathematicians, historians, and artists. We also want them to learn to be responsible participants in a democratic society and care about justice for all people, not just themselves. The school is often the first place children learn to participate in a society beyond the home.

Those of us who have been teaching for more than ten years usually note the gradual erosion of this focus. First, more and more responsibilities that used to be handled within the home have been given to and accepted by schools. The topics of drug abuse, domestic violence, child molestation, smoking, and AIDS have been added to curriculum. With both parents working or with mothers who are raising children by themselves, parents are also struggling to nurture and educate. This usually means the lines of responsibility are blurred and the focus begins to waver.

When schools assume roles that have traditionally been allocated to parents, teachers have no choice but to enter into more of a paternal or maternal role. The percentage of children who arrive at school not fed, clothed properly, emotionally upset, or distracted is rising. For the sake of that child's learning or for the sake of the learning community, the child simply cannot be ignored. By default or by adoption, the main business of schools has changed dramatically from a central focus on learning to a broader nurturing, community-building role.

How Do You Make a Profit?

For many, politicians in particular, the profit in education is represented in better scores and beating the norms. A single number representing profit or loss in a child's life, school system, state, or country does not adequately represent what should be the bottom line for learning and profit. Educators have to redefine the meaning of profit at all levels. Numbers *can be important* and are not to be ignored. Current definitions of profit, however, only measure convergent thinking, the student's ability to process another person's thinking. Profit also has to be thought of in terms of child initiative, the ability to create and write, sustain long-term thinking, and solve problems cooperatively with others.

How Does Your Competition Make a Profit?

We often compare American schools to the schools of other countries. In some areas, especially in science, mathematics and languages, Americans lag behind in test scores and performance. But our competition stays open for business much longer than our own American schools. The school day in Europe and some Asian countries can be as much as two hours longer. In addition, their school year is 210 to 220 days, or 40 days longer than our 180 days. Their curricula are more classically and academically oriented for a more select population. That is, we educate a broader range of students for a longer part of their lives than do countries overseas.

American students, although testing lower than foreign students in science and mathematics, have demonstrated a kind of innovative entrepreneurship with both ideas and technology that has set them apart from students in other countries. American initiative and breaking with tradition is one of our trademarks. I don't believe we have recognized the power of these elements in our culture. They are certainly one of the prized elements in our intellectual currency. Sadly, in current efforts to boost scores the time students spend in innovating and exploring new ideas is often given short shrift.

Similarities Between Teaching and Other Occupations

Teaching has more in common with other occupations and professions than I understood at first when I began my study in November of 1998. No question, teaching is unique because it involves the lives of children and students. But most of the factors that create energy in other occupations contribute energy to classroom teachers as well.

Creative Edge

People derive energy when they feel that there is some creative edge, usually unique to themselves, that they exercise in their work. For example, a stock broker discovers that women often have a fear of the market or have never had responsibility for a sum of money they can call their own. The broker organizes women's groups and helps them gain confidence in understanding the language of the market or how to sustain their new-found confidence through investment. A physician discovers a new surgical procedure. "It's that breakthrough thing," the doctor reported. A real estate broker listens to a client speak but deduces from the negative what aspects the client really wants in a home. A marketing person senses a need in the market, pitches an advertisement in that direction for a product, and notes a rise in sales. The creative edge taps into the energy generated by discovery. It is usually important that the proponents of the new procedure be free to break from tradition and have the support of their employers. Of course, some people have enough self-confidence and energy to form their own companies or change jobs where the freedom to create and express new ideas is encouraged.

It is essential that teachers have the same freedom to create. The energy-filled teachers are continually creating new materials, investigating new approaches, or revamping the ways they use time. The teaching life is filled with the constant need to adapt. In one sense, teachers are creating new products and procedures to fit the learning lives of children nearly from minute to minute. The teacher prepares in detail for discovery and then adapts.

The Learning Journey

I asked a physician how often she consults with other doctors. "I'd say at least twenty to thirty times a day," she replied. "There is just so much to learn. And that's after twelve years of study and two years in the field. There is the research, new drugs, and procedures. It is hard to maintain the big picture as well as the detailed information that is constantly coming in. My decision has to cut to the heart of the matter." In this instance the doctor was speaking of the scientific side. Then there is the individual patient, what the patient presents as symptoms, emotional state, and the ability to learn in order to negotiate a successful course of treatment. There is hardly any field or occupation that isn't presented with an exponential growth of information, as well as clients, and customers who are also beset by more complex problems.

Mentors

I was struck by how many people in other occupations spoke of mentors, or colleagues who were of immediate help to them. If they didn't mention them by name, they lamented how much they needed them. If the mentor was not nearby, they consulted by e-mail, or took a mental trip back to a scene in which mentors of years ago might have handled a similar situation today.

Of near equal importance to being mentored is mentoring. Teaching or helping someone else is an important part of learning. In short, we learn by teaching and increase our energy by giving to other human beings. One CEO of a company stated, "I want every one of my employees to know something well and to be able to pass it on. There's a different energy in a company that does that."

People who have energy are constantly giving it away. Energy begets energy. Janet Tassel in her article, "Yo-Yo Ma's Journeys," in *Harvard Magazine*, reports from her interview:

> Many of the students' questions involved stamina and endurance. "Go with the energy around you," he [Yo-Yo Ma] urged Lauren, who, having just played the prelude to the cello concerto of Eduoard Lalo, was concerned at how drained she felt. "I used to get very tired from playing this movement," he reassured her. "Use the power of the orchestra to help you, that's the secret. Save a little, so you can give a little more. You have to expend energy in order to produce energy. If you empty yourself, you're going to fill yourself even more."

Teachers need access to each other. Although they may not need to consult in as much detail as physicians, they are still faced with complex cases in learning and behavior. They wonder about the best uses of resources and procedures. This is especially true of new teachers who still need mentors to carry them along. Even more, they need mentors and administrators who have a realistic sense of professional growth over a three- to five-year period. Consider Jane Fraser's book, *Teacher to Teacher—A Guidebook for Effective Mentoring* (1998), as a help in this area. I find that many new teachers are expected to maintain the same statistical child growth on standardized tests as other professionals with twenty-five years of experience.

Knowledge as Energy

In setting up an interview for this study with a physician I got the curt question, "What are you studying and what are you going to ask me?"

I replied, "I'm studying human energy in the workplace and I have an opening question, 'What gives you energy, takes it away, and for you is a waste of time?'"

"That's easy," she replied, "When I know what I'm doing I have energy, and when I don't know what I'm doing, I don't."

I said, "That's a heck of a good beginning but we do need to talk more." We continued to talk and the physician said, "I read an article, consult with a colleague, conduct an examination, listen to the patient,

138

and put many things together to come up with an accurate diagnosis. That's very uplifting. You did a good job. You made the right choice."

She went on to say that not all knowing is clear on the surface. "Medicine is such a complex thing and it is a science and theoretically the right answer does exist. I've studied and studied through medical school and residency and beyond, but medicine is much more of an art with only some basic scientific principles to guide you." The art is in making the right choice based on the melding of science and the patient.

Again and again, people spoke of the energy of knowing. In most cases they were applying a lifetime of knowledge to new situations, first cousins of old problems but configured in a different way. A software designer visits a company manager who wonders if she can design a software that will handle complex problems in multiple billing to fit their way of doing business. The designer melds what she knows from her own boilerplate softwares and reconfigures them to fit the new company. Energy from creating, learning, and applying sound knowledge is generated in the programmer.

An office manager expressed it differently: "I need to work smarter but not harder. I set up our computers to give data that we really need. That's the constant challenge, to not waste time and be unproductive." Time is so precious in the lives of many companies that a better data source will save time and be an energy giver in its own right

Knowledge is a great source of energy for teachers. A teacher draws on his or her understanding of linguistics and language as well as the child's reading process to formulate the next approach to helping the child to read. Study, experience, and a knowledge of the child contribute to the artful decisions the teacher makes. Indeed, teaching is the artful melding of many sources of information. Teachers literally make hundreds of such decisions throughout the day. As in medicine, I'm sure teachers would utter the same words as the doctor: "When I know what I'm doing I have energy; when I don't know what I'm doing, I don't." This is why beginning teaching is very difficult; it is so hard to draw on the energy and experience of real knowing.

Teachers also generate energy from "working smarter but not harder." They know when to delegate to children and others. They also have a repertoire for showing children how to do things instead of telling them. Smart teachers know what types of teaching last.

139

Time, Control, and Energy

My informants continually spoke of the energy of being "lost in time." They became so absorbed in what they were doing that they felt fully used and immersed in the task. It often came from intense concentration. Mihaly Cszikszentmihalyi, former chair of the department of psychology at the University of Chicago, has done studies of humans as they concentrate. His findings report that people in deep concentration produce endorphins, the same chemicals produced by runners who run long distances, and often referred to as a runner's high. Deep focus produces energy.

For some workers, the chance to take on one project that will absorb all their energies without interruption is an energy-producing event. The supervisor says, "I need you to stop what you are doing now, and take on this extra assignment. You are the one person who can do this job; turn off the telephone and go work." In one sense this is the ideal energy-generating event and an invitation to deep, uninterrupted thought. Two factors have come together to produce the ideal work situation:

1. You are the person for the job.
2. You will have control of time and task.

I find that teachers who have longer blocks of time and have been able to reduce both internal and external interruptions are able to produce greater concentration in their teaching. Equally important to the teacher's concentration is the child's. Children need to "get lost" in their work and that often happens when they are exploring and discovering whether in experiment, the depths of a book, or a piece of writing.

Clear Goals

When everyone in a business or institution has a clear sense of direction, the energy flow is less diffuse and more easily directed. Employees are usually able to answer quite clearly the basic questions posed by my neighbor in Scotland: "How do you make a profit, how does your competition make a profit, and what business are you in?" Further, the reward structure through bonuses, salary, and advancement are clearly connected to the goals of the institution.

Teachers and educators need clear goals as well. Unless educators can state clearly their business and help a staff to focus responsibly and responsively to goals, there will be much wasted effort, confusion in the staff, and the drain of discouragement, even anger. Although reward structures cannot be worked out quite as clearly as in business, the examples provided by Virginia Secor and many of the Maine situations show the fruits of clear goal constructing. As in business, the carefully developed language to discuss the product (children's learning) is an essential in staff energy and vision. Clear goals make up the vision that a system has for both teachers and learning in the students.

Knowledgeable Evaluation

I interviewed a CEO of a hotel chain who spoke of the reward structure he used with people handling reservations from the front desk. "We have ten criteria that ought to be covered in handling a reservation," he said. "That's because our research shows that a successful reservation includes these. Every one of the desk clerks knows what they are. Two or three times a month we listen in to a transaction. If at each of those times we listen they hit all ten of the criteria, all the clerks working that month get a $100 bonus. Of course, we know that all the clerks will be most diligent in making sure everyone else handles the reservations by the book."

This is a rather mechanical example of supervision. The criteria for handling a telephone call are clear-cut and the evaluation fits the criteria. Not all jobs lend themselves to that kind of evaluation or supervision. Nevertheless, the criteria by which people will be evaluated have to be spelled out between management and the workers. When interpretations of the meaning or efficacy of procedures require more objective interpretation then dialogue has to follow. Evaluation with dialogue can be energy giving. At the heart of successful dialogue is the expertise of the person doing the evaluation. The supervisor has to be expert in the knowledge of the position, as well as skilled in conducting the dialogue. Both are necessary. In addition, the criteria have to be applied to a longer-term curve of development for sound growth for both the employee and the employer. Part of an evaluation includes a review of where the employee has been, where he or she is now, and the joint formulation of new goals. Many businesses are fortunate in having bonus systems attached to performance as well as profit sharing and stock bonuses connecting the employee to the overall success of the company.

Teachers are usually dependent on the principal or immediate departmental supervisor for the setting of joint objectives and a system of direct observation. In some cases a system of peer evaluation is included along with the administrator's. There is no greater energy giver than an effective evaluation. Teachers need to have a sense of where they are professionally. Day after day, they put their emotions and knowledge on the line. Although they have student data that confirms in a rough sense how the day to day work is going, every professional wants to improve and needs outside help to maintain a professional vision. There is so much art in teaching that every conscientious teacher is usually aided by another set of eyes and a strong listener.

Common Energy Drains Between Teaching and Other Occupations

The fundamentals of what drains energy similarly cut across most occupations. The people I interviewed seemed gleeful in unloading their pet peeves. In some cases, the problems were serious drains that stole energy from valuable work time.

Staff Meetings
High on the list of "waste of time" statements for all occupations was the staff meeting. I have been on both sides of the issue, as both leader and participant. Another professor and I moaned about departmental faculty meetings at lunch one day and decided that we'd conduct a little research to help us pass the time. We chose a series of variables to monitor:

1. Who spoke and how often
2. If the person spoke did it have anything to do with what the last person said
3. What other activities were people doing that had nothing to do with the meeting? (Reading, writing, talking to people next to them, laughing asides)

The staff meeting seems to represent a ritual in American democracy that is a near plague to all. It serves as a reminder of some of the imperfections in a democratic society. Danling Fu, soon to be an American citizen and formerly from the People's Republic of China, loves her new country but wrings her hands at the endless discussions of little consequence to advance business in a democratic society. Rather than moving toward common goals, people are protective of their own territories and niggled over wording to make sure their identities were maintained.

The purpose of this chapter is not to diagnose or solve the meeting problem, but I find that most people do not feel an important part of the meeting. The issues under discussion often have little to do with the main purpose of the business and do not actually require the thinking of all participants. There are many kinds of meetings: the informational meeting, the policy meeting (formulating new directions), and the problem-solving meeting. The length of meetings is also a problem. The chair, supervisor, or CEO usually knows that people are impatient and tries to cut off extraneous discussion. Unfortunately, items that may require more lengthy discussion get tabled and do not get enough time to arrive at a successful solution. The most common complaint is with the informational meeting. "Why couldn't this just be written out for us to read?" the group members lament. "Because you don't read," snaps the leader.

I know a school principal who began faculty meetings with a student reading aloud a piece of writing, sharing an art piece, or telling a learning story. "I don't ever want the faculty to forget what we're here for," she said. "It affects what I put on the agenda and serves to channel our discussions more productively." Schools tend to have top-down items on their agendas. That is, there are policy issues from the superintendent or board that are passed on without discussion and are for information only. They are shared to emphasize their importance.

Liberal Use of the Word Crisis

Rapid, accelerated growth in all aspects of American life both in government and business, as well as in the personal lives of employees, produce crises demanding rapid response. Listen to the evening news on radio or television and the word *crisis* is used liberally. Examine the meaning of *crisis*: "A crucial point or situation in the course of anything; turning point." The derivation is from the Greek, *krisis*, meaning "turning point." Unfortunately, the word *crisis* is used to call attention to problems for the sake of selling newspapers, and increasing their Nielsen ratings. It seems that everyone has crises: patients, athletes, students, CEOs, the elderly, unions, foreign governments. Communication is so rapid and immediate that I wear an international skin sensitive to the vicissitudes and crises of a troubled world.

It is fashionable to speak of "the crisis" in American education. Instead of saying improvements are needed, the speaker uses *crisis* as a shout word. "Hear me, hear me," the speaker says, "things have never been worse in education." David Berliner and Bruce Biddle (1996) and others have documented quite clearly how education has continued to improve even as it has sought to educate more people from all levels of society.

After a while, people no longer respond to the word *crisis*. They are drained by the sudden mustering of energy for the fifth crisis in a row. Their feelings grow dull. When a true crisis does arise, it is difficult for them to respond. Leaders have to be selective with their choices of words. Above all they need to have a response system from all facets of their business that allow people to speak of problems at the grassroots level. If issues rise gradually and early enough from the lower echelons responses can be given before major problems will arise. Unfortunately, top-down management structures beget more crisis citations as a means to spurring greater production and maintaining control over the employees.

Disgruntled Employees

Working next to unhappy employees who create a negative atmosphere was high on the list of energy drainers. "I was having a good day until Joe walked in," one employee said. "And Joe didn't have to say a word. He just carries an unhappy history. When he does speak, I guarantee his first words will have a negative edge to them. It could be the weather, his wife, the company, or the lousy coffee in the office. Things are just never right."

People give energy but they can take it away just as quickly. Sometimes the source of the drain is outside the company: an illness; a bad marriage; an unruly adolescent; or a sick parent. Conversely, I have seen people who have the same list of problems yet have boundless energy and an optimistic outlook. Somewhere early in life, they gave difficult problems a different translation. They see themselves as problem solvers rather than victims. They refuse to accept the guilt that is sent their way and see those persons who levy the guilt as the ones having the problem, not themselves.

A classic case is Robert Coles' story of the African American girl who had to walk through a line of spitting, cursing white people when she tried to enter the school during the days of court-ordered integration. Coles noticed that the girl's face was one of calm. As a child psychiatrist, Coles wondered how children could handle the trauma of angry white people assigning a negative status to them. When he interviewed the little girl, he realized that the girl saw the white people as having the problem.

Unclear Goals, Fuzzy Job Descriptions, and Incessant Interruption

All three of these interrelated items were frequently mentioned as energy drainers. When company goals are clear, good job descriptions usually follow, and the institution has a clear sense of what promotes productivity.

When companies cannot articulate what business they are in with clarity, the place of each person in the company is unclear, and frustration abounds. A sense of vision and participation is lost. Frustration is soon replaced by anger and counterproductivity. Although interruptions are somewhat normal in any business because of the increased complexity of human needs, they break the concentration required for deeper and more demanding thinking. Interruptions are symptoms of poor planning. We live and work in a time when availability is often up front in company advertising. But how available do we want to be and still be productive?

Forms and Paperwork

As society has become more complex and litigious, more people need to know what we are doing. We fill file cabinets full of records just in anticipation of a review by another body. As fast as we design computer systems to reduce the load, more is added. Federal, state, and local governments require records for taxes, compliance with workplace safety, human rights, ethnic makeup, product safety, and so forth. Companies hire extra personnel who specialize in handling such demands. But even the specialists have to get our data, and we resent the time and distraction paperwork (or computer work) takes away from our normal business.

When I first began teaching, I maintained a daily attendance register, kept records of student grades, and filled out an annual book and supply order. That was the extent of my annual paperwork requirement. Today teachers write special reports referring children for reading, special education, speech, various therapies, as well as write extensive letters describing children's progress. More people need to know more about our children than ever before.

Production Goals—Two Cases

Most people I interviewed, especially those who evidenced the characteristics of high energy, were articulate about how they used time and worked toward greater productivity. I share two cases for discussion of the issue of production goals. Sometimes high production goals can undermine production or produce distortions in employees' lives that may cause greater problems in the future.

In a number of my interviews I asked the question, "On a scale of one to ten, how do you rate your energy level?" I then followed with three more questions: "What makes it a six or seven?" and "What would you have to do to make it a ten?" or "Do you know someone who is a ten? Tell me about that person."

An Entrepreneur

I interviewed a chief executive of a software company on a flight between San Francisco and Chicago. After a discussion about his business in which he said he was in the air about twenty days out of thirty from his home base in Chicago, he said he'd place his energy level at an eight. "What makes it an eight?" I queried.

"Well, I carry my office with me." He showed me an expanded briefcase complete with telephone, computer with attached modem, compartments with software, and literature. "No matter where I am, I'm available. I have not only instant contact with my Chicago office but with matters of troubleshooting, I can handle it all right here," he said as he patted his briefcase. He went on to tell how rapidly his company was expanding with new offices in Philadelphia for banking, another in San Francisco. His company had recently gone public in the stock market and shot up rapidly in the first months. "God knows what I'm worth now," he said with a touch of pride. He then paused to say, "What goes up can come down just as fast and that market out there is vicious with companies that don't show a profit," he said wistfully.

"What would you need to do to go from eight to ten?" I asked.

"There is a guy I used to work for who has his own company now. Same business. Never sleeps. He just doesn't seem to need sleep. He lives the business and is so dedicated anyone near him just wants to do the same. It's almost thrilling to be around him. He'll go far. I need more sleep but I'd like to have the same effect on the people around me." Occasionally, the CEO, a young man in his mid-forties, talked about his son. "I call him on the telephone each day and see him maybe one weekend a month, sometimes two." I asked him to tell me about his son and he spoke about the thirteen-year-old's talent with computers.

A University Professor

I interviewed the next case at his university office. This late-fifties gentleman was a leading researcher in his field, chair of an important department in the university, very active in campus affairs, and a leader in working with the state legislature for the benefit of the university. He met me early on a May morning the week after spring commencement. We met alone in the empty building. He was dressed casually and sat relaxed in his chair. He spoke about his work.

"I've known for years that I'm overcommitted. I have a terrible time saying no, especially when I'm really interested in something. I'm never caught up but I'm more relaxed about it than maybe I ought to be. I seem to be able to do high-quality work at the last minute. But I'm not a type-A personality. My Dad was and it drove me crazy as a kid. Somehow I have pieced together time so that I allow myself to do fun things." *Balance* was an important word in his discussion. "I love to play golf and I go running every noon." He was passionate about his work, listening to his colleagues, and especially about his long-term commitment to the future of his university. "What keeps me energized is thinking about the future. I tend to be an optimist to a fault. But I think it is an enormous strength. Nothing is impossible. Having a plan energizes me."

I asked him where he placed himself in energy level on a scale of one to ten. "I'd say about a seven or eight," he replied. "And what would you need to do to make it a ten?" I asked.

"Oh," he said with a smile, "If I went for a ten I'd lose my seven or eight. That would mean I'd lose my balance, my fun, and my energy. I'd no longer have the seven or eight."

A key question is, "At what point does productivity begin to regress with overwork and unrealistic production goals?" A still greater question is, "When does productivity interfere with your own articulated vision for what you want to give to life including family, coworkers and friends?"

The issue of productivity in teaching is ever at hand. We know that our work is never done, especially when we feel a responsibility for the young lives in our classroom. We can always do more. Earlier in Chapter 2, we took stock and in Chapter 3, we set a personal and professional direction. We acquire energy by giving energy but sometimes the giving is not done smartly and time and energy are wasted.

The Uniqueness of Teaching

I have deliberately reviewed energy givers and drainers in other occupations to show how much we have in common. School administrators and boards often forget that we experience the same issues and problems as in other occupations, but because we are schools, important workplace matters are forgotten. Indeed, our workplaces and conditions need reexamination, especially in light of what adds or takes energy from our main focus, the children.

Yet there is something distinctive about teaching as an occupation. You may have felt a pang of envy in reading about the clear connections between production goals, profits, and rewards at business. I'm sure you are aware that there are business and professional people who leave their companies and higher salaries to teach in public and private education. Profit became such a high priority that some people left because they wanted to invest in young lives rather than material goals. The notion that their business was connected to people was too distant to have immediate effect on their lives. As one respondent answered, "I began to resemble my product and it was dulling my mind."

Yes, teaching is an emotional roller coaster because our business is the growth of human beings. We willingly bring our personalities and emotions to the fore and invite children into learning. The child can stamp his foot and say a loud "no" or strike another child over the head with a block. Sometimes the responses are hostile and personal, and we may feel temporarily demeaned by parents and the administrators who should give us support.

When teachers have control of time, space, and resources and the freedom to expect more of children, the energy is returned many fold. Teaching is called a profession because the professional in that classroom has studied, experienced, and learned about that particular group of children. It is a profession because it is centered in the well-being and growth of its clients, the children. There is always a need to improve and we need to be challenged. As professionals, however, we expect to be heard and to challenge in return. Perhaps people have forgotten we are a profession because we have not fought hard enough on behalf of the children.

13

Principals and Teachers Build Energy

I was appointed principal of an elementary school forty-two years ago. I was young, inexperienced and alternated between naive over-confidence and sudden terror. In my first three months as principal, a teacher had a mental breakdown, children smashed a bank of school windows, a drunken parent waved a gun in the school lobby, a teacher shut a child in the closet, and the chairman of the ways and means committee for the Parent–Teacher Association spent the cake-sale money on food for her family.

My principal had shielded me, a teacher, from the everyday realities of what confronted school administrators. I took the place of a well-respected administrator, and inherited a staff with only two teachers who had less teaching experience than I did. I worried that the staff would yearn for the good old days with the former administrator. Beset by the wave of unanticipated problems, I moved into a kind of survival mode. I was self-conscious, somewhat defensive, and thought more of how to control the staff than to assist and lead them. My style was reminiscent of Garrison Keillor's description of Mr. Detman, the principal from Lake Wobegon, "He lived as if a giant icicle hung over his head."

My managerial style (not unlike my first year of teaching) was a mixture of authoritarianism and permissiveness. Letters to the faculty and parents were cryptic and authoritative: "The legal limit for being eligible for riding the bus is 1.0 mile." Unfortunately, the line fell between two houses that were 100 feet apart. I stuck to the letter of the law amid loud, protesting voices; one rode, one walked. I was proud of my control. I knew nothing of diplomacy. On the other hand, I tried to make allowances for some respected faculty members, while being more severe with new staff members. An excellent assistant principal and a wise custodian helped to chart me through the murky waters of that first year.

Instruction was my specialty. I demonstrated new ideas from first through sixth grade. I pushed for change, *my* change. Although I didn't mandate the changes, the staff had little doubt about what I wanted them to do. I reasoned that it was a principal's job to get people to improve their teaching. I suspect that if the era of extensive standardized assessments was in vogue in those days, I would have been first in line to insist on raising standards through testing. I preached teaching to individual differences through leveled reading, variant learning rates, and social needs. Of course, I ignored those tenets when dealing with the faculty, never thinking that staff also had different learning rates, variance in experience, and social needs.

A few of the faculty reluctantly tried my new approaches to individualized learning. Most, however, greeted me with silence in the corridors. Conversation in my faculty room lapsed into conventionality: "Damp weather, do you suppose we'll have afternoon recess? How are the kids? How is Betty?" They wondered what to say. Our separation was palpable. I could feel it in my stomach and the weight across my shoulders. My vision was not their vision. I didn't know how to help us help each other toward a common goal, the learning of children. We were fatigued but for the wrong reasons.

Schools Change

Schools have changed dramatically in forty years, and the principal's role has expanded exponentially. My 420-pupil building had fourteen classroom teachers, a custodian, secretary, assistant principal, and three cafeteria workers. We had no trouble finding a place to park our cars. Today our parking lots are overflowing with double the staff: reading, speech, English-as-a-second language, special education, and learning disability specialists. There are teachers for physical education, art, music, guidance couselors, teacher interns, and parent volunteers, as well as aides. With increased numbers of staff, schedules become more complex and require constant adjustment. These are all people a principal must bring together to work toward a common goal, and each of these professionals requires time to confer about learning.

The Role of the Principal

I've asked some veteran principals about changes in the last twenty years that require more of their attention. Independent of a growth in curriculum there are school safety and legal issues. The two are inter-related. Parents and professionals know that the children are more vulnerable to health hazards (smoking, drugs, alcohol) and human dangers (molestation, divorce, custody battles).

Principals must meet a stream of parents who expect to have a greater role in school practice and direction. A diverse range of parents speaking different languages, from multiple religious and ethnic groups, arrive wanting to move their children to another teacher, help with homework, teach their children to read, or volunteer in classrooms. Some are concerned about their child's depression and fears. Parents argue about curriculum. Some want more emphasis on the arts, some less. One principal said, "I expect to be a buffer between parents and teachers. I see myself as handling the first impact of contact to put a better frame on things. Sometimes parents arrive at flash point. Maybe I can listen and hear their concerns. I think of this especially with new, beginning teachers of whom we have so many."

Today parents expect to have greater influence in our schools than they did forty years ago. Except for a few informal meetings with the Parent–Teacher Association and a smattering of conferences, in earlier days parents let the schools do the educating. Now principals have to provide knowledgeable leadership to include parents in the education of their children, as well as help them to understand shifts in curriculum and new ventures.

Experienced principals made other comments about changes in the last twenty to thirty years:

Resources and standards: Today we have more resources, and great knowledge about kids learning, the brain—all of that. Some of the standards stuff is pretty good in that you can see what is essential in learning. But standards go awry when standardization accompanies standards. We try to make all teachers and kids the same. It won't work.

Curriculum: There's just so much of it and much of it is good. We've got to do a better job with the faculty in selecting what is essential in curriculum. You can't teach it all and we're going to kill the new teachers

152

entering the profession because they don't know how to select wisely. They try to do it all.

The classroom: While our resources are better, the square footage in our classrooms and the time we have to work in them is unchanged in the last fifty years. We bring in science materials, math manipulatives, children's literature, and computer stations. When the kids work they need to spread out the materials. No business would tolerate the kind of work spaces our teachers and kids have to work in. Teachers try to counteract the time/space problem by working longer hours. When I leave at 5:00, a third of my staff is still here working.

Learning: The good news is that today we know all children can learn. Even if they come from a dysfunctional home, we do know how to teach them to read, even with no home support, or even if they are hungry. There can be a tendency in a high-poverty school to believe differently. And that belief system is pernicious. It may take more time but we can teach and they can learn.

Principals are educators in the middle. They are in the middle between boards of education, their superintendents, parents, and teachers, each with their emotional demands requiring response from the principal. Memos and letters arrive on paper or electronically via Faxes and e-mails. Principals could shut their doors and remain in their offices just to deal with the paperwork and communications. Principals who are the educational leaders of their buildings leave their offices and walk the corridors to be with students and teachers. They instinctively know that their main source for energy lies where the learning is taking place. Of necessity, principals have learned to delegate responsibility in order to continue to learn themselves and maintain touch with the vision.

I have visited buildings where principals and teachers share a common vision. Each provides energy for the other. On the other hand I have been in buildings, not unlike my first responsibility as a principal, where teachers are isolated, separated from their administrators, and pulling in many different directions. Principals can do things for teachers and teachers do things that will help principals.

One of the best examples of a principal in action is Shelley Harwayne, former principal of the Manhattan New School. You will

153

want to read *Going Public* (1999) to view a unique blend of teacher initiative, broad-based literacy, in an ethnically diverse neighborhood. I have walked the corridors with Shelley and listened to her informed conversations with each child she meets. Faculty meetings are filled with individual teacher contributions with knowledgeable discussions about children and learning. Each professional approaches teaching in their own way yet all share one vision in common, a love for children and their learning.

Building a Vision

Teachers and principals create energy for each other when they are in the process of shaping a vision together. The vision is centered on children's learning. When both administration and faculty place an unwavering focus on what constitutes learning in the children, then there is a constant source of renewable energy. Indeed, we can tell when the focus is wavering because we see each other instead of the children. We worry about ourselves, our own needs, and begin to find fault with each other.

Vision building is slow, thorough work. The *American Heritage Dictionary* defines vision as: *the faculty of sight, that which is or has been seen, unusual competence in discernment or perception; intelligent foresight*. Vision building is hardly a dreamy affair; rather, it is rooted in the specific and it is in the specific that the sense of possibility grows.

Begin Small

Choose an aspect of curriculum where there are common needs, but needs that are easily identifiable: spelling, writing, language conventions, or mathematical problem solving. These cut across all the grades and are not too difficult to assess. The point in choosing a limited, locally determined curriculum need as a focus is that it will become the laboratory for learning to create a vision of possibility for children's learning. The staff needs to participate in each phase of growth from choice of curriculum area, to inservice, scheduling work sessions, approaches to teaching, and evaluation design. Once you have a successful model in place you can move out to other areas of the curriculum. The staff has to see the fruits of local initiative.

Vision building begins by developing our perceptions and competence in discerning learning in children. I'll choose a simple area as an example, children's use of conventions in written language. It will be necessary for the staff to have children keep all their writing papers in portfolios. Unless there are collections in any curriculum area you choose, you will not be able to monitor change or tell if there is progress. Further, the collection will be the laboratory for vision making and developing discernment with the staff. I recommend that the principal and other staff members without classrooms link with a specific classroom member to make up a team. For example, the principal may link up with a second-grade teacher and the physical education teacher with a fourth-grade teacher, and so forth. Here is a series of meetings to show how the process is carried forward. It is very similar to the one used by Virginia Secor in Chapter 11. The basic principles could be used as guidelines for any curriculum area you may choose.

Session One
Question: What are the data? How do children use conventions in each grade level? Everything a writer does in writing is an act of convention from putting spaces between words, correct spelling, words and letters moving from left to write, indenting, or punctuation marks to help meaning with the sentence. See Graves *A Fresh Look at Writing* (1994) pp. 191–210. Choose folders of three children, a suspected high, middle, and low learner, and list which conventions these children use accurately from at least three papers, and which conventions they've *attempted* but have not used with consistent accuracy.

Session Two
Post the results from session one by grade level. Look at the data of what the children *do know, what they are attempting to show,* and discuss what is possible. Begin the business of vision making and teaching from these data.

Session Three
Consider two demonstrations with children to show the process of helping them discern which conventions they already know. See pp. 193–194 of Graves (1994) *A Fresh Look at Writing.* It is very important that children be part of vision making. We always begin with what they discern they already know and then move to the new. These demonstrations are done in the "round," with the faculty viewing the process.

155

For discussion: What do the children know? Hypothesize about what they could learn next.

Session Four
Share the data about what children discern about conventions from the various rooms. Begin teaching conventions within the context of their own needs. Children should begin to keep lists of what conventions they know, and ought to know. Develop and circulate various mini-lessons from staff members in the building.

Session Five
Develop a vision of what might be possible in six months or a year. From time to time, bring children into the workshop from various grade levels to explain about their knowledge of conventions and what they hope to learn next.

A Review of Principles
1. Vision making comes from the specifics of what children know now and could learn. This is not a deficit approach but a careful look at where the children are today. We look for potential.
2. All staff members are involved in gathering data, reviewing data, and hypothesizing about future data.
3. Children are partners in gathering data, discerning what they know, and need to know. If children aren't part of the vision we lose out on the energy we need to sustain each other in learning.
4. Specific lessons and games are developed and shared to help the data change.
5. Staff develops their own ongoing measures and decide their frequency for determining progress.

Remember, you have chosen a small, easily attainable aspect of curriculum to begin to learn about vision building. Notice how much discussion there is about children and their potential as well as the full sweep of what children do from year to year.

Staff Involvement
Choose an area for vision building that includes the interest of as many of the staff as possible since all staff are involved. Obviously, some instructional specialists are quite unrelated to the area you have chosen. As much as possible, draw on staff expertise to move the project ahead. A diversified leadership is the best possible situation. Of

course, the presence of the principal in all of the workshops is essential to helping the staff learn how to build a vision for the school.

Other Approaches to Building a Vision

I have interviewed many principals across the country about building a vision for their schools. Here are four very different approaches from four successful administrators. Vision building has to fit local situations as well as the leadership style of the principal. Look for the common strands among their statements. Each statement is made by a different principal:

A. You ask everyone for where they want to be three to five years from now. You ask for individual visions and really get into the learning process. You look for common strands that cut across individual visions. You make a decision that will help everyone and then focus. But you can't just have a vision in isolation of the district. It is the principal's responsibility to keep your vision in touch with what is happening elsewhere. You can't be isolated because you will come to a point where you are going to need resources to carry out your vision. Everyone has to buy into the vision and you do this gradually. You aren't going to get 100 percent of the staff to start with. It is interesting in that you aren't as much into nuts and bolts as you are into the core values the staff holds together about kids and learning. So, you start small and gradually expand the vision. That's what vision is, expanding through excellence.

B. Our vision began when there was a core group who said, "There is no excuse for children not learning. We acknowledge that what they have in life is not that great but it doesn't excuse us from not teaching them to the best of our ability." You see, we had to change our language and our conversations. The language changes this way. Before we'd say, "Jose isn't reading yet but what can you expect from his situation?" Now we say, "Jose isn't reading yet but we've got to find a way." And we have; our scores have gone way up.

Parents have to be part of the vision. I meet parents who walk with their children and I'm out there when they come after school. I invite them in to talk about expectations. I'll drop anything to talk to a parent. Every parent knows what we expect and they also know we need them to be part of it. The local newspapers have caught on to what is happening. It's a different place here. Now we are generating our own energy. There's a passion here based on results. We refuse to accept the word, *can't.*

C. I try to keep the vision simple and that doesn't mean it isn't deep. Trust is a big part of any vision. You don't suddenly storm in and say, "Let's have a vision." You have to earn the trust of the teachers in that they know it is okay to make mistakes and the roof won't cave in. That's part of teaching and learning. You can't try new ventures without tripping. There are core values about trust between administration, kids and teachers that have to be in place. Too many places look to packaged programs to build visions for learning. Well, I say they can't get there that way. Packaged programs try to bypass teachers and their judgments. Visions have to be homegrown, gradually developed, and based on trust.

D. I think it is important to do a lot of talking and listening. I would advise a new principal to make some key value statements about kids right up front. Say what they think is very important, what they believe, and how they make decisions. Make it clear that you don't have a blueprint but all kids can learn. In my case before I came there was like a press conference with the faculty. They asked me lots of tough questions. One questioner asked, "How do we get rid of disruptive kids?" First, in answer I had to show that I understood reality. I said we had to build our capacity to deal with them. There will be some kids we can't for reasons of safety. But any time they leave we'll mourn and wonder what we could have done differently. You have to find opportunity to make statements like that. Again and again you have to show in good contexts, with real problems what you mean. This is what good teachers in the classroom do all day long.

Principals Help Teachers Build Energy

I visited a school recently where each Wednesday morning the faculty met to have a breakfast of rolls, juice, and coffee and then moved into various curriculum focus groups. The faculty had one half hour together before school and then one half hour after the children arrived on the buses. The staff ran the sessions and discussion groups. "I have but one requirement," the principal said, "that everyone attend and no one be alone in their room. I make sure the kids are in a good situation for their half hour. I often read aloud to them, or

158

they'll have a video, or I bring in a storyteller from the outside. Every June we reevaluate the Wednesday morning program and decide what specific interest groups will follow for the next year. In previous years we've produced lots of things: parent forums, the new math curriculum in the early 90s; we prepared a language arts presentation for parents." This particular program has been going for ten years. There is renewal for the staff in the middle of the week and, above all, keeps the staff in touch with each other and develops new ideas.

Again and again, teachers speak of the ways isolation drains their energy. This is especially true for first- and second-year teachers who seem to be more isolated than others. When principals deliberately plan time for teachers to be together or set up mentorships for aiding new teachers, energy is created for both the person helping as well as the new professional.

I asked teachers what administrators did that gave them energy. Their responses had remarkable consistency:

- "I'd like my administrator just to see what I'm doing. I need another set of eyes. He wouldn't have to evaluate but just say, 'I see this and that.' "
- "I'd like specific feedback not just say, 'Nice job.' I mean that's okay but I'd like the details."
- "It means so much when an administrator, or anyone else for that matter, asks you for advice. It could be about most anything."
- "When my administrator sees me as having something unique to contribute to the staff or others and asks me to do it. Sometimes I don't want to because I'm too busy, but it is nice to have a good reputation."

The top principals who had strong relationships with their staffs were generally out of their offices and available to their staffs on an informal basis. They identified with the business concept of "management by walking around." They usually arrived at school well before the teachers, dealt with the necessary paperwork, and then were out and around in the corridors, ducking into rooms, encouraging first-year teachers, and generally feeling the pulse of the building. Whether a teacher actually had contact with the principal was

159

secondary to just seeing an administrator give knowledgeable encouragement to the staff.

One principal focused on a language of invitation to both children and staff. She wrote a letter to the faculty once every week and a half, showing with details what she saw that was positive. In addition, she wrote a daily letter to the children that she posted on an easel at the front entrance to the building. When I visited the school, clusters of children paused to read what was new about the building, current events, or the weather. Often the daily news asked children questions. The principal spoke with delight as she showed many of the notes she received about "morning news" from the children. This principal knew the value of her effect as everyone entering the school encountered a focus on children and the world around them. Of course, they began their day with reading. She also wrote a letter to parents that was translated into two languages with their language and English in a side-by-side format.

Principals would do well to analyze the language they use in their memos to staff, children, or parents. Is it a language of specific observation as well as one of invitation? Underlying any communication is the unspoken question, "Who does the author of this memo think I am?"

Teachers Help Principals Build Energy

Many times, it is in the teacher's self-interest to keep principals informed of progress in their classrooms. For many years, I have recommended that teachers schedule an interview for the second or third week of October in order to begin to show administrators the early growth in the children. This is especially important if you are trying new approaches to learning. You show from the outset that you are geared to progress and evaluation. You will want to maintain collections of work from the opening of school so you can show which children are doing well, or who are moving more slowly. This will establish a reference point of *your* choosing for the remainder of the year.

Administrators and supervisors are always in need of information. Don't forget that your immediate supervisors also have people with whom they want to share data about progress in the school. Consider bringing three full collections of work from different levels of learners in order to show the details of progress. Show the child's progress by pointing out the details you consider important. Administrators don't often have access to real learning as they have to deal more globally with an entire school.

If you are fortunate enough to be in a building where there is a clear sharing of vision between administration and faculty be sure to articulate your student's progress by sharing data related to the vision. I find that teachers who take the initiative to inform get a different exchange of energy than those who wait for the administrator to come to them.

Increasingly, principals are exchanging e-mail messages with the faculty. Find out if your principal wishes to have that kind of communication. State up front how you wish to use the medium. E-mail is especially helpful because it allows both teacher and administrator more flexibility in maintaining contact. Keep the e-mail, as well as personal contacts, focused on the children. If further resources or extra help with learning are needed continue to relate them to what children need. Through e-mail and personal notes, share important events from your classroom. Principals may not have time to fully respond and your notes may be "for information purposes only," but send them anyway. If you keep your memos and e-mail notes in your computer file, you will have a good record of your correspondence through the year.

Reflection

At the end of one of my interviews a principal remarked, "A good principal does just what the best teachers do."

"What's that?" I asked.

"They work to build class spirit and help everyone to help everyone else. Teachers are constantly delegating and putting themselves out of a job to focus on the important business at hand, learning. They aren't afraid to ask the children for advice on a better way to solve a problem. They know their kids and the strengths and weaknesses of each. Best of all, the kids know the teacher knows them. In one sense, the teacher is the chief learner in the room, so they keep showing kids how and what they have learned. The best teachers are good administrators. And I guess the best administrators are good teachers."

14

Explore More Lasting
Sources of Energy

Emily had a decision to make. She arose early, turned on the coffee machine, pressed her skirt and blouse, and checked the weather on TV. Last night before she went to bed, the weather reporter was on the fence about a snowstorm arriving midmorning the next day. She wondered if Jack Morey, the meteorologist scheduled to visit her fifth-grade class, would be held up by the storm. She chuckled because he, too, was uncertain yesterday about the storm. A storm meant that he'd be at the station all day preparing for a late-afternoon broadcast. The class had been preparing for the visit as the culmination of their unit on meteorology. Good news: The weather report this morning showed a storm delay, meaning her visitor would be with the children.

She walked into the bedroom to awaken her three-year-old daughter, Jennifer. She reached over, and gave Jennifer a light shake. "Time to rise and shine," she said cheerily. "Ummm," Jennifer moaned and then coughed. Several times Emily spoke. A moan was Jennifer's only response. Emily reached down, picked her up in an embrace and felt a hot cheek against her own. "Uh oh." This was not the warmth of the blankets, but a substantial fever. "Wouldn't you know it, Jennifer gets sick whenever Roger is off on a trip."

Her mind raced. She could wrap Jennifer in blankets and take her to Nicole, her accomplished sitter. "Thank God for Nicole," she whispered to herself. Last summer when she'd been desperate to find good day care, her close friend Nicole had decided to take in an extra child to be with her own daughter, one year younger. But how could she send the sickness on to Nicole's own daughter? Emily thought of her class. After all their preparations, she'd miss the children's excitement and questions after hearing Mr. Morey. She took a deep breath, made her decision, lifted the telephone, and called the substitute hot line.

"Mrs. Pressman won't be in today. Please arrange a substitute, grade five. I'll call the school with extra details." She could have postponed Mr. Morey's visit; she'd miss the excitement, but she knew the children would be just as delighted to tell her all she'd missed. She pondered her decision again, "Yes," she thought, "I'm a mother who happens to be a teacher." Emily was decisive. Decisive decisions are energy givers.

We balance our lives between school and home every day. Even if we are not married or have children, we go home to a world that beckons with its choices. Sometimes we are so busy in both worlds that we aren't conscious of any separation. How well I recall a Saturday morning pushing my half-filled cart around the corner of an aisle in the supermarket and meeting Tony, one of my students. I remember the surprise on Tony's face when he said, "Mr. Graves!" He was startled to meet me but also to find I had an existence apart from school. He examined the cereal boxes, dairy products, and produce in my cart and looked up with an unspoken judgment, "You even eat food!"

Jane Hansen tells the story in *When Learners Evaluate* (1998) of asking her students to speak of themselves as educators. One of her students, Becky, brought in a collage showing herself as a mother/educator of three adolescents. Jane thought that Becky misunderstood her university assignment until she considered the importance of what her student had done. "Her life as a teacher and mother is just that, a life. She doesn't lead two lives. She spends much mental energy integrating the two and when they fit together, life works. When one has to be kept in a closet she feels inner conflict—and, probably outer conflict." Jane made an additional point to me on e-mail when she said, "Somehow we don't honor both lives—or see both lives as one cohesive life. And, thus, we don't see the value in students' out-of-school lives, either!" Indeed, we lose an entire curriculum and, as Jane suggests, we project our own experience into that of our students.

To this point, we have focused mainly on the issues of energy drain as well as energy sources in the school. But we all experience energy sources and drains in our life beyond the school. Each world affects the other, and in this instance I want to deal with principles and practices that help both worlds of home and school. In Chapter 2 you did a careful analysis of both worlds when you carefully put

163

down everything you did and then analyzed those episodes for energy giving and taking and waste of time. You made some decisions about the direction of your whole life and not just your career. You had to be good at saying "yes" and "no" as well as what you wanted more of and less of.

Home–School Transitions

INVITATION: *Focus on transitions from school to home and home to school.*

We are constantly switching worlds. Perhaps the greatest switch is the school–home transition. I find that transitions take more planning than expected. There may be many different types of errands before you actually arrive home: take your son to music lesson, daughter to Little League practice, go grocery shopping, pick up a prescription, or pick up your infant from child care.

I laugh now as I recall my rides home from school or university. I rehearsed the idyllic scene that would greet me when I walked through the door. Reality struck when Betty or the kids would be waiting with their lists of problems or things they wanted me to do. Just as in conferences and challenging questions, we need to take deep breaths before we enter into home life. We need the ten- to fifteen-minute break when we walk through the door. The need for the break can be explained, but unless we hold to it, it won't be allowed.

I find that the break can take many forms: Sip a glass of wine and listen to your spouse talk about his or her day. Listen and observe while your son or daughter shares a drawing. One teacher works in his garden. "There's just nothing quite like putting your hands in soil, or participating in the growth of living things," he says. He goes straight to his garden the minute he gets home. Side-by-side walking is another kind of transition. Walking and talking work very well together, even though you may feel on the verge of collapse. I find that light motion is often a better transition than falling into a chair. Enjoy a light jog alone or with others.

Some of my study participants had their way of making a transition while driving from school to home. One said that she thought about school driving to school, but then switched on the way home, rehearsing what she'd do with her son, how they might ride bicycles together. Another kept a notepad on the dashboard and made notes about what he'd do at home. One question I didn't ask but wished I had was: "Do you notice any difference in your driving to school versus driving home?" I wonder about the need for a more relaxed pace while driving home. Many teachers listen to book tapes or enjoy music on their CD players. Another says he sings at the top of his lungs to accompany his favorite music on radio or CD.

Integrating Our Lives

INVITATION: *Take time alone to consider the integration of both your lives.*

I find that many teachers rise before the rest of the family if they happen to be morning persons. Those who aren't morning persons, choose to be alone late in the evening after the children have retired. I was impressed by how many high-energy teachers were comfortable with being alone. The source of their energy seemed to come from stepping out of the rat race to write a journal, keep a diary, pray, do yoga, or meditate. In short, they quietly worked at transcending themselves in space and time. I laughed when Anna Quindlan, the novelist, said in a commencement address, "Remember if you win the rat race, that means you are still a rat."

You may be a list maker like myself. I even have a slick little Palm V computer on which I can carry an electronic "to do" list, maintain my calendar, addresses, and a host of other facts. The busier I get, the longer the list. Just putting something on the list or into my computer gives me the feeling that I am in control. But the list may control me. I have to have a strong sense of personal direction in order to say, "No, this doesn't belong on the list. It belongs to someone else or isn't even worth doing." This is where the time alone is so important. This is where we learn to save time by not doing what may well be a waste of time. It is also our place of renewal, the place to build peace in the maelstrom.

Work to Put the Past to Rest

INVITATION: *Put to rest problems from the past that interfere with the present.*

I asked an optional question of many of my participants: "Tell me about four or five things you've been carrying in your mind for the past five years and you wish they weren't there." In some cases, people were carrying guilt over students whom they felt they hadn't reached. I certainly carry my list of students. I don't dwell on them but they exist. Many carried burdens for sons and daughters, marriages that didn't work, or parents in nursing homes at long distance from themselves. Still others wondered if their cancer would recur, worried that they couldn't stop smoking, or wished they could lose weight.

I remember a meeting nine months ago with a group of teachers in a small school in Maine. Except for myself, all of those attending were women. One asked, "What are some of the things you've learned in your energy study?" I mentioned that some teachers carry such large burdens I wondered how they could get out of bed in the morning in order to teach. I added a quick observation to the data, "And most of these people are women who carry unusual burdens of guilt."

The teacher quickly snapped a reply, "That's because the men don't carry any!" We laughed and I've pondered her statement ever since that summer day. At the risk of overgeneralizing, I think that most women are more reflective than men. I noticed that fact when I did my study of sex differences in seven-year-old children nearly thirty years ago. The ability to reflect also allows the person to consider her own behaviors more thoughtfully. My study showed that young boys lead more of an external journey with greater exploration of space as well as more comparative, competitive statements.

I explore the guilt territory because an overwrought sense of guilt tends to make us overcompensate by taking on more responsibilities than is helpful to our own well-being. I certainly find myself accepting engagements simply because I owe the person a favor rather than considering what might be best for the person who is asking. Quite apart from guilt and responsibility is an overly developed ego that says too quickly, "That's right, I *am* the only person who can do this." I remember moaning about canceling an engagement because I was still getting over the flu. My close friend Don Murray's wife, Minnie Mae, wryly quipped, "They'd have no trouble canceling if you were dead!" I also find that many men and some women are overbooked for competitive reasons. We are in a constant, never-ending process of building our resumes.

For me to say, "Stop visiting the scene of your guilt," is like asking you to stop thinking of a purple cow. I find that people who take guilt questions and write down their specifics already begin to put them to rest. Some are significant and complicated enough for us to seek professional help. I have done this several times during my life and found it to be particularly helpful.

An important step is to increase our contacts with others. Give the burdens some light and fresh air. Most people know how to choose the one person whom they know is the good listener. On the other hand, there may be some events that are so painful we need to have a knowledgeable professional to help us. If we feel some burdens are too great and they are draining us, then further help may be needed.

Let Work at School Help at Home

INVITATION: *Consider practices that work at school and apply them to other areas of your life.*

There were many practices I did in school that worked very well. Unfortunately, I'd forget them the minute I arrived home. I was good at listening to children with personal traumas or those who had difficulties with other children. My classroom was well organized and I'd delegated many responsibilities in order to build a community.

I remember Mary Ellen Giacobbe, the remarkable first-grade teacher from whom I gathered research about teaching writing. When children came to her asking for help with a problem, personal or academic, she usually responded with a question, "I hear you, Mark, and I'll bet you've already starting thinking about the solution. Tell me what you've thought about so far." Usually the children have thought about it, and do know the solutions to most of their problems. When children know that Mrs. Giacobbi will ask the question, they automatically begin their rehearsal before meeting with her.

167

I regret to report that I've often forgotten that what worked in school could just as well work at home. We need to consider transferring many of our good teaching practices to other aspects of our lives. Consider applying at home some of these good teaching practices:

- *Delegate.* We worry that we may not do enough for our children because we work. Our children, husband, wife, and anyone else living in our home need to become part of the team and assume responsibilities. Children take care of our room in school and they also need to do the same in our own household.
- *Demonstrate.* If I delegate responsibility, I have to show family members how to take over specific tasks. They either work next to me or I demonstrate until it is clear to both of us that the task can be handled independently.
- *Listen.* This was always my Achilles heel. After listening intently all day, I took shortcuts at home and dictated without listening. I'd answer too quickly and give solutions. Good listening works at home and at school.
- *Ask questions.* Ask people for solutions. Respect the fact that children, friends, husbands, and wives have already thought through many issues. We may not agree with their solutions, but we do need to listen.
- *Work together on common projects.* We build classroom communities by helping others beyond ourselves. Working on common projects for others means we need each other in order to succeed. The end is not ourselves, but others beyond the room or household. Usually, this means that everyone has a skill to contribute to building a family feeling.
- *Laugh.* Classroom communities know how to laugh because everyone has a place and a responsibility. People are secure enough to laugh at themselves, especially if the teacher is able to do so. Education and family matters are too serious a matter not to laugh at our pretensions as we seek to do the near impossible. Read aloud from humorous stories in school and at home. There is no greater energy giver than laughter.
- *Set limits.* No classroom, family, or individual life can function without setting limits. Most limits are negotiated, but some are

not. Safety limits are nonnegotiable. I will carefully explain the reasons for safety limits as in responses to strangers, range of territory allowed, use of bicycles, visitors inside the house when I am not at home, and automobiles. Health also has its limits in terms of junk food, TV watching, and bed times. Of course, we set limits knowing they will be challenged at home as well as in school. There are also negotiable limits within the health areas since there are often exceptions. The challenge is to allow as wide a range of choice as possible for our family that we may learn the meaning of effective choice.

I work hard at orchestrating these policies in my classroom. I may not be able to suddenly institute all of them at home or in my activities beyond the household, but I can begin to plan slowly in order to experience the same energy at home as I do with students in school. The good news may be that I may have more decision-making power at home. Choose then your beginning point and enjoy the fruits of new energy. Remember, this has to be a guilt-free trip. These are opportunities, not assignments.

Love as Power

INVITATION: Consider the meaning of love, commitment, and material attachments.

There is nothing quite like the energy of love. I easily recall those first days of falling in love with my wife, Betty. The notion that someone could love me in return was mind-boggling. There was spring in my step, the sun was brighter, and the moon more wondrous. It was as if the world was new, fresh, and could be rediscovered all over again. The love stayed fresh until we began to "remake" each other into our own vision of the perfect mate. I laugh now at my immaturity. But I figured that sooner or later Betty would see the wisdom of rising at 5:00 A.M. and planning every minute of the day. She thought the same: "Why couldn't I be more like her father who spent more time around the house and could fix things?" There isn't any couple or close friends who can't list the differences in the other as well as the similarities. I laugh at the line from Pygmalion, "Why can't a woman be more like a man?"

169

Women will utter a similar line, "What I really need is a wife!" Fortunately, Deborah Tannen (1991) helps us understand male and female differences more clearly today. But love does not seek to alter.

Naturally, there is enormous energy in loving our children; yes, even in adolescence. The energy is in the giving: the changing of diapers, the lunch-box surprises, helping with homework, laughing with them, playing games, and picking them up out of the dust when they have fallen for the third time learning to ride a bicycle. The loving is also in the limits we set and the challenges that come to those limits. We work hard to help them think for themselves, never realizing that they will first practice that brash independent thinking on us. Our household is the safe laboratory for their experiments in independent thinking. But sometimes it gets very, very noisy.

Recently, I began an arduous undertaking, sorting through six large boxes of several generations of photographs and artifacts. I felt like a museum curator as I visited the faces from previous generations. I studied their faces and those of my mother and father when they were young, just married, and having children. I felt a wave of sadness because they had died, but then I realized how lucky I was to place myself in the stream of family history. Think back to the invitation in Chapter 2 when we looked back and then looked ahead. Keeping the big picture in mind, and feeling a sense of gratitude for those who have come before us, is an energy giver.

Reexamine Multitasking

INVITATION: *Review the multitasking aspects of life outside of school for their energy-giving and energy-depleting contributions.*

One of the characteristics of modern life is multitask living. Gleick (1999) portrays it as doing several things simultaneously. As I write this chapter, I am listening to the *Brandenburg* concerto and occasionally checking the mountains for the first onset of snow coming down the valley. It's almost as if I can't just write. Worse, a month ago while reading Gleick, I was watching the Lehrer *News Hour* and listening for the weather on the FM radio while eating supper. Betty was seated next to me, reading her book and catching the news. Occasionally, we'd stop and comment about the news or weather. Sometimes I've counted as many as four things I'm doing simultaneously and not necessarily doing any of them very well.

I suspect that our children, and especially teens, are even better at multitasked living than we are. For their lives and our own, the key word is *option*. We press our daughter for what she'll do on Saturday night. "I don't know," she says.

I reply, "Oh good, then maybe we can go out together."

"No, no," she says, "I need to keep my options open." Her implication is that something better might come along.

I'll admit that music definitely helps me to write. I'm not listening to it, yet it sets a certain mood for me to enter into myself. I'm beginning, however, to question multitasked living. It means that so many of my experiences are watered down. I don't enter into them fully and therefore miss out on the benefits of being consumed by the event. I don't experience the flow of full participation. I end up being a taster and not a liver. My problem is commitment and reducing my options in order to experience the full energy of one event. I have a hunch that our children, who are so used to multitasked living, find that focusing on just one paper, or one book, is more difficult than we might imagine.

We are well acquainted with interruptions in school, but the home provides no guarantee of sanctuary. Telephone calls, Faxes, computers, and beepers make us available to the world, but at what price? I confess that I find most phone calls disturbing. Most want me to do or buy something. But I have to remind myself that I am in charge and can take specific steps to reduce the barrage: I can turn on the answering machine or unplug the phone.

Diet, Sleep, and Exercise

INVITATION: *Review diet, sleep, and exercise options as important contributors to your energy level.*

There are times when our emotions seem to demand more food than we need. Often the food we choose is the wrong kind. Unfortunately, I gravitate to sweets, breads, and fatty food as a false reward for my hard work. Satisfaction is temporary and within hours I'm eating again.

When I am emotionally drained I tend to exercise less unless I have a regular discipline of walking, running, cycling, aerobics, or stretching. There is nothing like the healing power of motion to drain off stress and emotional upset. Many of the high-energy people I interviewed had some kind of mild exercise program. The key is that it was regular and they were disciplined enough to do the exercise at points of high fatigue. Some even used the words, "I'm so tired and stressed I've got to work out. I don't feel like it at all. I feel like slumping into a chair." They had exercised enough to know that no matter how poorly they felt, they'd feel better afterward.

Exercise and balanced eating are strong contributors to restful sleep. If your sleep is disturbed review your eating and exercise habits.

Create — Renewing Our Energy

INVITATION: *Review the places in your life where you feel you are actively creating.*

The act of creating has to be looked at in its broadest terms. I refer to creative living as artful living. Georgia O'Keeffe, the famous artist, expressed it this way when she taught art to her students in public school in Amarillo, Texas (Lisle, 1986):

> When I teach my main point is not to teach them to paint pictures but to show them a way of seeing. When I teach art I teach it as the thing everyone has to use. There is art in the line of a jacket and in the shape of the collar as well as in the way one addresses a letter, combs one's hair or puts a window in a house.

I discovered Georgia O'Keeffe when writing *Bring Life into Learning* (1999). In fact, it was the act of exploring what brought life into the classroom and across the curriculum that gave rise to my study of professional energy and this book. When I explored the artist and scientist's way of seeing and discovering, the importance of those events as energy giving came to the fore.

Artful living begins with a new way of seeing and appreciating. This is accompanied by artful doing. Artful doing begins with tak-

172

ing the most routine acts each day and throwing in a different twist. I say to myself, "This time I will vacuum using a different pattern. I'll go around the edges and keep coming to the center of the rug instead of going in parallel lines. When I shave I'll start on the left side and start at the top, instead of the bottom; or I'll brush my teeth a different way." I watch myself and the process as I experience the newness.

Some of our artful ways are less transitory. Open a cookbook and use a recipe you have never cooked before. Retrieve an old piece of furniture from the attic or basement and give it a new place in your home. Rearrange your garden flowers. Take five minutes just to sketch a vase. Sketch rapidly just to appreciate the lines in the vase.

Like the teacher who went straight to his garden and experienced renewal from the earth, go to a workplace you've created, a well-tooled work bench, a sewing center, a box of paints, the piano, or take out an unused guitar and begin to play. Sit among your collection of stamps, dolls, postcards, old bottles. Pick them up and hold them, rearrange them, and create a new order.

Artful living is an endless source of energy. It is an endless source because we are in the process of seeing and making the world anew. At the same time we create new lives for ourselves. We look at ourselves differently and consequently look at other people differently.

Artful living resists categorical thinking and is in the constant process of taking down artificial walls that define human territories. The artful liver is in the business of making new connections between things, between people, and knows no ownership of territory or things. They view their possessions as one of temporary custodianship to be used responsibly and passed on to the next generation.

Act on Decisions

INVITATION: *Make a list of decisions that have been pending for at least three months and begin to act on them.*

Pending decisions take energy. With the passage of time, the pending decision begins to occupy a much larger portion of mental activity than it deserves. Pending decisions seem to grow in importance and produce a sinking kind of lethargy just to think about them. No question, some decisions do deserve a waiting period, and may require long-term thinking. Without deciding which decision requires waiting, make a list of which decisions are occupying more space and energy than they deserve.

The way back to recapturing energy from decisions that are motionless is to first give them specifics. Take your top six items and write about each for no more than five minutes. You are looking to give each of them rich detail. When pending decisions sit like vague menacing blobs on the horizon they are especially debilitating. We give them light and bring them near with specifics. I'll take two of my own and write for five minutes about each:

> I've been fussing with what to write when I finish *The Energy to Teach* for about six months. I've written three books without a break and I need a change of pace—I think. I'd like to get back to writing poetry. I like the high focus of ten lines or so and I think I'd like to get back to writing more poetry for children. I need something for the short haul, not the long haul. But then I've got two books in manuscript form, *A War Comes Home* and *The Eye of the Whale*. It makes me sick to stare at those two manuscripts on the shelf and do nothing. I gave each a full year of my life. Oh well, it sounds like the poetry is still the best way to get back.

> I've been postponing a visit to my aunt, my mother's sister, for some time. Why do I avoid setting up a time to see her? I know I'll be doing nothing but listening, but I need to listen for she has much to say. I need to see her for her sake as well as my own. I've uncovered photos that only she can identify. She's eighty-seven and they'll be lost to the ages if I don't make the trip. I need to set up a time on my calendar and just take the time for the four-hour drive.

Notice that I try to not only get into the details but also to bring in the emotions associated with my indecision. I could begin to feel the actual decision I'd make as the five minutes on each was coming to a close.

There is rarely a time when decisions are crisply made. The art of following through on decisions is the art of making repairs as we go along. I decide to revise my novel, *The Eye of the Whale*. I know that my opening scene needs to be more in the center of the action than leading up to it. I will head out in the general direction of rewriting the scene. I'll need to make many changes I can't anticipate. That's the way it is with craft and living. Mozart could carry entire scores in his mind and then just put them to paper with hardly any revision. But few of us are Mozarts. A committee decides to set sail on a new venture, but most assuredly, as new information is unveiled in the realization of the project, adjustments will have to be made. A person once said, "The course of any great ship is one of many tacks."

There is no greater energy drain than the defense of intellectual categories, an overly wrought protection of possessions, or an ego-inflated defense of one's sense of authority. There is energy in giving away, and creating anew with others, and the delight of temporarily possessing something that gives pure joy in the moment. Strangely, if I think the object is mine "forever" I lose out on its gift today.

Reflection

A psychiatrist friend, Dr. Rob Richardson, and I have been walking a mile-and-a-half circuit in the center of Jackson every Wednesday for the past three years. We bounce our theories and passions off one another, construct charts, and share writing. Quite naturally the subject of human energy has entered into our discussions. During our last walk, Rob spoke of the "drain of not enough" in our culture. There's not enough time with our clients, friends, spouses, or children. Then there's not enough money, land, friends, or not a good-enough car. The tragedy of the drain of "not enough," we agreed, is our loss of gratitude and opportunity, which is a never-ending source of energy.

We need to turn around the rhetoric of "not enough" in education. Take energy from what our students bring, knowing every day that our students do learn. Let us sharpen our perceptions in order to see what they have and what our colleagues have to offer. No question, we need to expect more, but our expectations are based on what we see in them, rather than what is missing. Day after day we will expend smart, well-placed, caring energy. It is in the giving of energy that energy returns to us.

References

Allen, Camille. 2001. *The Multigenre Research Paper: Voice, Passion, and Discovery Grades 3–6*. Portsmouth, NH: Heinemann.

The American Heritage Dictionary of the English Language. 1973. Boston: Houghton-Mifflin.

Archer, Jeff. *Education Week*. March 17, 1999.

Berliner, David, and Bruce J. Biddle. 1995. *The Manufactured Crisis: Myths, Fraud, and the Attack on America's Public Schools*. Reading, Mass.: Addison-Wesley.

Calkins, Lucy, Montgomery, Kate, and Santman, Donna. 1999. *A Teacher's Guide to Standardized Reading Tests*. Portsmouth, NH: Heinemann.

Cassidy, John. "The Price Prophet." *The New Yorker* Vol. 75, No. 45, p. 44.

Csikszentmihalyi, Mihaly. 1990. *Flow—The Psychology of Optimal Experience*. New York: Harper and Row.

Covey, Stephen R. 1989. *Seven Habits of Highly Effective People*. New York: Simon and Schuster.

———. 1999. *Living the Seven Habits*. New York: Simon and Schuster.

Falk, Beverly. 2000. *Getting to the Heart of the Matter*. Portsmouth, NH: Heinemann.

Fraser, Jane. 1998. *Teacher to Teacher: A Guidebook for Effective Mentoring*. Portsmouth, NH: Heinemann.

Gleick, James. 1999. *Faster: The Acceleration of Just About Everything*. New York: Pantheon.

Goleman, Daniel. 1995. *Emotional Intelligence*. New York: Bantam Books.

———. 1998. *Working with Emotional Intelligence.* New York: Bantam Books.

Graves, Donald H. 1983. *Writing: Teachers and Children at Work.* Exeter, NH: Heinemann.

———. 1992. *Explore Poetry.* Portsmouth, NH: Heinemann.

———. 1994. *A Fresh Look at Writing.* Portsmouth, NH: Heinemann.

———. 1999. *Bring Life into Learning.* Portsmouth, NH: Heinemann.

———. 1998. *How to Catch a Shark and Other Stories About Teaching and Learning.* Portsmouth, NH: Heinemann.

Hansen, Jane. 1998. *When Learners Evaluate.* Portsmouth, NH: Heinemann.

Harwayne, Shelley. 1999. *Going Public: Priorities and Practice at the Manhattan New School.* Portsmouth, NH: Heinemann.

Kohn, Alfie. 1999. *The Schools Our Children Deserve: Moving Beyond Traditional Classrooms and "Tougher Standards."* New York: Houghton-Mifflin.

———. 2000. *The Case Against Standardized Testing: Raising the Scores, Ruining the Schools.* Portsmouth: NH: Heinemann.

Lisle, Laurie. 1986. *Portrait of an Artist: Georgia O'Keeffe.* New York: Washington Square Press.

McCullough, David. 1999. Fall. "The Art of Biography II." *Paris Review.*

Ohanian, Susan. 1999. *One Size Fits Few: The Folly of Educational Standards.* Portsmouth, NH: Heinemann.

Rogovin, Paula. 1998. *Classroom Interviews.* Portsmouth, NH: Heinemann.

Routman, Regie. 2000. *Conversations: Strategies for Teaching, Learning, and Evaluating.* Portsmouth, NH: Heinemann.

Tannen, Deborah. 1991. *You Just Don't Understand: Women and Men in Conversation.* New York: Ballantine.

Van Hayek, Friedrich August. 2000. *The New Yorker.* Vol. 75, No. 45 (February 7).

Index